The **POWER** Series

ISRAEL'S AIR FORCE

1948 to Today

Samuel M. Katz

Motorbooks International
Publishers & Wholesalers ®

First published in 1991 by Motorbooks International Publishers & Wholesalers, PO Box 2, 729 Prospect Avenue, Osceola, WI 54020 USA

Motorbooks International books are also available at discounts in bulk quantity for industrial or sales-promotional use. For details write to Special Sales Manager at the Publisher's address

Library of Congress Cataloging-in-Publication Data
Katz, Samuel M.
   Israel's air force / Samuel M. Katz.
     p. cm. — (The Power series)
   Includes index.
   ISBN 0-87938-534-0
   1. Israel. Hel ha-avir. I. Title. II. Series:
Power series (Osceola, Wis.)
UG635.I75K38 1991
358.4'0095694—dc20   91-11013

Printed and bound in Hong Kong

On the front cover: *One of the IAF's deadliest assets is the F-15 Eagle. This one is credited with the destruction of six Syrian aircraft.* Michael Giladi

On the back cover: *Along with state-of-the art aircraft such as the F-16 Fighting Falcon, the IAF protects Israel with indigenously improved F-4 Phantoms, A-4 Skyhawks and AH-1 Cobras.* BITON HEYL HAVIR

On the frontispiece: *A pair of F-16s patrol the skies over northern Israel.* BITON HEYL HAVIR

On the title page: *With an F-16 driver playing spectator, an IAF Phantom makes its dramatic and ear-splitting lunge toward the heavens.* BITON HEYL HAVIR

Contents

Preface

As I sit here at my desk, gazing in awe at a color glossy of an Israel Air Force (IAF) C-130 Hercules on takeoff, I realize that any book on the HEYL HAVIR, the Israel Air Force, could never be complete. The IAF's role in defending the Jewish State, preserving its aerial integrity, and being on the cutting edge of Israeli military operations, be they routine or spectacular, is a continuous process. From Beirut to Baghdad, Tunis to Damascus, Ras Arab to Rachadiyeh, the IAF has always been there for the State of Israel; with the Middle East maintaining its tinderbox status, the IAF will have to be there for the State of Israel in the future, as well.

The true story of the Israel Air Force is a tangled maze of personal dramas, high-flying feats, and self-sacrifice and dedication. No one book, especially one of this limited size, could ever hope to encompass the zeal and devotion of the gentile volunteers who, after flying and escaping death in World War II, were the IAF's first pilots during the dark days of 1948; nor could it describe the courage of those who flew a most daring sortie far from home to destroy the Osirak nuclear reactor in Baghdad, Iraq, an operation that saved the Jewish State from a mushrooming apocalypse. With this book I hope to give a human face to the IAF, to give it a realistic identity, and to show the pilots, technicians, and conscript-soldiers not as supermen and superwomen, but as mortals with a mission; they are men and women who must be better than anyone else simply because they have to be. Anything less might mean disaster.

A book on a complex, self-sustained, and familylike military force, like the IAF, could never materialize without the help, friendship, and good faith of a great many people. I offer a heartfelt TODAH RABAH, "thanks," to the IAF attaché in Washington, for his support and assistance; the IAF's Public Relations Office in Israel; Israel Defense Force (IDF) spokesman Brigadier General Nachman Shai; and Lieutenant Colonel S. at the censor's office for his quick and fair review of my manuscript. I also thank a talented group of photographers: Yuval Navon and the crew at the IDF Spokesman's Photographic Unit; Michael Zarfati of the IDF weekly magazine, BAMACHANE; and the high-flying shutter snappers at BITON HEYL HAVIR, the IAF magazine, headed by Gil Arbel.

I would also like to thank a few friends and family members for their gracious help, generosity, and ability to put up with a demanding author. I offer my sincere gratitude to four friends: Andreas Constantinou for his skilled touch at turning undeveloped film into publishable material; Dan David and Joe Ward for keeping their eagle eyes always on the lookout for useful material; and Yoav Efrati, whose love for the IAF is expressed in his work and hobbies, for his desire to see this book through. Most important, I thank three family members, without whose tireless troubles this book would not have been possible. Many thanks to Nissim Elyakim for his tenacious efforts in and out of the censor's office; "Shiri" Elyakim for her faithful archival work; and, last but not least, my loving and patient wife, Sigalit. Sigi was involved in every aspect of producing this book, from typing letters to the IAF's "who's who" in Hebrew, to turning an unidentifiable pile of slides into orderly material suitable for publication.

Samuel M. Katz
January 1990

Chapter 1

Introduction

The breathtaking sunset of October 16, 1986, was deceiving in its tranquility and beauty—it was, after all, appearing over chaotic Lebanon. As the sun began its descent out of the mountains in the east onto the shimmering waters of the Mediterranean Sea, several high-flying aircraft began their dive in from the south. They were F-4E Phantoms of the Israel Air Force (IAF), aging workhorses that had served and saved the State of Israel in three major wars, over eighteen years of incessant combat, preemptive military actions, and countless retaliatory antiterrorist bombings. On that sun-baked Lebanese afternoon, the Phantoms were out on a routine bombing mission against Palestinian terrorist targets in the Miyeh-Miyeh refugee camp just south of the ancient port city of Sidon in southern Lebanon. The ensuing evening, however, would turn out to be anything but routine.

As the Phantoms began their menacing Stuka-like dive onto the target, barrages of 14.5 millimeter projectiles hurled toward the sky by both Palestinian and Lebanese Shiite gunners began heading their way; these factions are usually at war with one another, except when an Israeli warplane becomes a unifying target. The IAF warplanes have proved impervious to such ground fire, however; according to foreign sources, they have used phosphorus flares as decoys to the heat-seeking target acquisition systems of handheld antiaircraft (AA) missiles such as the Soviet SAM-7 and the American Stinger, or pure pilot skill and aircraft maneuverability to outchase, outsmart, and outluck the hails of hostile AA fire that usually greet them. With the Phantoms surpassing the threats from the ground, the day's targets, a series of terrorist shore-based gun emplacements and fishing vessels used to launch amphibious attacks against northern Israel, appeared clearly in the bombsights of the aircraft.

The planes released several bombs in the run, but the lead Phantom suffered a most unfortunate accident at a most inopportune time. As the pilot pushed his bomb-release button, an electronic malfunction in the aircraft's triggering mechanism caused one of the bombs, a 500 pounder, to detonate. Within a millisecond, the once mighty Phantom was decimated by a thunderous, fiery explosion. Both pilot and navigator managed to eject from the inferno; they cascaded to earth amid a flurry of enemy activity and trails of illuminating tracer bullets. The routine of a Lebanese afternoon had given in to disaster. Tragedy could be averted only by desperate luck, unique skill, and, most of all, patience and courage.

According to the Phantom's skipper—who, in accordance with strict IAF security considerations, must simply be called the pilot—"It was like something from an old World War II movie. I was sure I was dead when I heard the loud BOOM and suddenly saw absolutely nothing—no electronic gear in the cockpit, no hands, no plane, nothing! There was an earsplitting bang...red flames...blackness...euphoric thoughts of mortality...and then the tug of the parachute!" As the pilot slowly slid down to earth, nervously gazing in a 360 degree radius for any sighting of his trusted navigator, he began to ponder his own precarious fate. Amid the chaos and confusion of his being shot down, the fear and pain of his wounds, the pilot thought about the horror and torture he'd be subjected to at the hands of a Palestinian, *Hizbollah* ("Party of God") or

Syrian interrogation. Suddenly, he thought of the family he realized he might never see again.

The pilot sluggishly flowed with the autumn wind on his path down to earth; he watched the red dusk of the Lebanese sunset turn into a dark blue and protective cover. The lovely and foreboding transition into evening was soon illuminated by hundreds of tracer bullets fired by the encroaching legions of Shiite and Palestinian gunners, each group desperate and eager to claim the pilot as its own. The glow from the automatic weapons fire rising toward the darkened heavens allowed the pilot to realize exactly what he was landing into: a deep *wadi*—a watercourse dried out from lack of rain and from heat—of thorny raspberry bushes and large boulders. Armed only with a 9 millimeter Beretta automatic, a handheld communications and signaling device, and the dwindling time of fate, the pilot realized that his meticulously cared for survival kit would not keep him from harm's way for long. It was every combat flyer's worst nightmare.

One thing that is apparent in Israel's military history is the nation's solemn oath promising that should its soldiers be captured, the army and government will do anything and everything to secure their release. Although the situation holds true for every Israeli serviceman and servicewoman, from a new infantry conscript-soldier fresh out of basic training to a high-ranking officer, the oath holds special significance for pilots. They are men and women of unique and special talents in whom the State of Israel has invested millions of shekels and whose knowledge and intimacy of top-secret operational procedure must remain in Israel at any cost. Moments after the pilot's Phantom erupted into a fiery ball of destruction, the wheels of the IAF's elaborate and effective integrated command and control apparatus were already set into high gear. While the pilot lay in pain on Lebanese soil, silently cursing to himself in the coarsest Arabic he could muster, help was already on the way.

Immediately after the Phantom was destroyed, other IAF warplanes were summoned to provide the pilot with some air support while a rescue operation would be attempted. At 1705 hours, at an air base somewhere in northern Israel, two AH–1S Cobra attack helicopters, the aerial vanguard of Israel's aerial antitank capabilities, were preparing to embark on a routine training exercise when they received word of the Phantom's downing near Sidon. The lead chopper was piloted by Captain I. and First Lieutenant A., and the second ship by Major A. and Captain H.; without fuss or lengthy procrastina-

Early morning flight time for an F–15, racing toward the heavens. BITON HEYL HAVIR

8

tion, they were ordered north immediately. They originally thought their mission would be one of support, perhaps to provide covering bursts of 20 millimeter cannon and TOW antitank missile fire to assist the rescue operation, while heliborne commandos from the IAF's elite Aeromedical Evacuation Unit (AEU) would pluck the pilot to safety.

For most other soldiers, starting the day in the safe confines of a training exercise and ending it in the midst of a combat operation is a shattering psychological experience. But pilots are a separate breed of soldier. With little fanfare, the Cobra crews checked their electronic instruments, ammunition count, and maps of Lebanon worn in clear pockets on their flight suit leggings and held their breath. Flying at a low altitude over Israel to preserve fuel and time, the two Cobras traveled 1500 meters (0.9 mile) out into the Mediterranean at the border

crossing of Rosh Hanikra, before heading northeast and into bandit country.

The pilot could do nothing but lay low and pray. With his coveted communications and signaling device betraying his position to only the IAF, he painfully crawled through the thick and thorny foliage and made his way to a covering pile of shrubs. Luckily for him, the two separate legions of Palestinian and Shiite gunners chasing him attempted to enter the deep and dangerous *wadi*, but movement was difficult and their progress was severely hindered. Steep rocky inclines were covered by unforgiving underbrush, and several Shiite gunners fell in their attempts to flush out the elusive pilot, suffering severe injuries. They nevertheless fired incessant bursts of 7.62 millimeter AK-47 and PK machine gun fire into the *wadi* and managed to get to within 100 meters of their prey.

Meanwhile, the pilot could only look nervously at his watch—30 difficult minutes had already passed—and begin to imagine what life as a POW would be like. Yet his anxiety was overtaken by confidence that the IAF would not abandon him and that his fate hinged on his own tenacity as a professional soldier and some very important patience, a trait Israelis—especially cocky pilots—are not famous for. Minutes later, relief did indeed come. The sound of enemy gunfire was soon muffled by the chopping and

An F–4E Phantom, flying evasively in the contested skies of the Levant. Gil Arbel, BITON HEYL HAVIR

A Cobra blasts away at a target with incessant 20 millimeter fire. BITON HEYL HAVIR

9

pounding beat of helicopter rotor blades, which materialized over the dusk-blackened tree line.

Radio contact was soon established between the Cobras and the pilot. As the Cobra crews attempted to determine the best and safest means of extracting him from the *wadi*, the pilot informed them that the Shiite gunners were closing in on his position and fast! There was no time to wait for the AEU, nor was there time to coordinate a secured rendezvous point where man and machine could meet. According

A re-enactment of the dramatic Cobra helicopter rescue of an IAF Phantom pilot from southern Lebanon, October 16, 1986. BITON HEYL HAVIR

to First Lieutenant A., "The possibility that the pilot would be captured obsessed my thoughts, and I knew we had to get him out of there. I hadn't yet decided on the technique by which we'd execute the rescue, but I knew we could do it and had to do it. I told my number 1, 'Let's go grab him,' and we entered into the *wadi* for either a heroic operation or a deadly encounter. It was like something I had read about in books on the Vietnam War!"

Unfortunately for the rescuers, the darkness, enemy fire, and deep and treacherous signature of the *wadi* made a landing at the pilot's feet impossible. As a result, Captain H. instructed the pilot to climb to the highest point of the *wadi* that he could reach and said the Cobra crews would take care of the rest. In the pilot's words, "Once I heard that they wanted me to reach an elevated spot, I realized that the rescue would be an eventful one. No ground force support and no AEU. It would have to be on the Cobra's landing skids! There was no other choice, and I believed that this was my only salvation. I was ready to leave the *wadi* on a kiddie's scooter if the situation called for it, anything . . . as long as I'd be flown the hell out of there!"

Climbing through a labyrinth of impassable thorny raspberry bushes and high, steep 50 degree cliffs, the pilot headed toward the agreed upon rendezvous point near a dangerously exposed slab of rock. The thorns tore deeply through his sage-green one-piece flight suit, and the first indications of pains from cuts, abrasions, and burns suffered during his ship's destruction became uncomfortably evident. Nevertheless, his short journey was successfully accomplished. A safe trip home seemed joyously imminent.

Yet as the two Cobras began their final descent into the *wadi*, the brilliant appearance of green and red tracers was followed by the telltale swishing sounds of automatic fire. The Lebanese version of heavy antiaircraft artillery—Soviet 14.5 millimeter heavy machine guns and 20 millimeter antiaircraft cannons mounted on crudely camouflaged Toyota pickup trucks—was brought into the fray. This hampered the Cobra's in-flight maneuvering and ability to jostle for position, especially with the fuel supply already running dangerously low. The Cobras let loose some quieting fire of their own, however, and attempted to conclude the operation without further incident.

In a risky maneuver, the two Cobras flew deep into the *wadi* in order to allow the ground fire to pass harmlessly above them. The pilot stood atop a rock and waved frantically toward the lead Cobra, guiding the rescue aircraft to his position with hand motions reminiscent of those used by a traffic controller at a major international airport. When eye contact was finally made with Captain H., the pilot was overcome by his anxious predicament and began to lose his stoic officerlike composure.

The original plan called for the number 2 Cobra to open its ordnance turret in order to allow the pilot to sit on top of it, but the crew and the exhausted flyer failed to coordinate the procedure; the incessant enemy fire made any protracted synchronization impossible. Sudden-

Perhaps discussing the latest advances in the Syrian Air Force or, more likely, the latest gossip on and off the base, two IAF corporals at an air base in northern Israel grab a quiet moment underneath the roar of supersonic aircraft. BITON HEYL HAVIR

The first F–16D makes its way to the IAF, courtesy of the US Air Force. BITON HEYL HAVIR

ly, as Major A. lowered his helicopter to approximately 1.5 meters above the ground, the pilot grabbed the bar that connected the landing skids to the helicopter's fuselage and held on for dear life. He positioned his arms around it and gripped with his armpit, pivoting his body to the ship in a secure fashion. With one trembling hand preciously holding the communications device, he shouted, "Let's go, let's go!" His screams, a boisterous combination of relief and sheer panic, were so loud that they were heard in the cockpit above the pounding beat of the rotor blades even without the communications device turned on!

As the Cobra began its delicate flight, the pilot looked up toward the pylons, only to notice the helicopter's seven-tube 20 millimeter rocket and the quadruple TOW missile launchers situated a foot above his head; he hoped that no one would shoot at him and that his rescuers would not be forced to fire at anyone either.

With the dramatic, almost comical, sight of the pilot dangling from the landing skids of one Cobra, the two helicopters carefully headed for home. The Cobras could not fly at optimum speeds, nor could they perform sharp and evasive maneuvers to avoid enemy ground fire. Against small arms fire, they would have to be lucky. Against a SAM-7, they were a large, slow-flying bull's-eye. The biggest fear was that an armed individual from one of the many small villages along the coast would spot the dangling

IAF Mirage IIIC number 111 is the master of six Syrian and seven Egyptian aircraft, all confirmed kills.

pilot and engage in a macabre game of "Lebanese target practice."

Captain H. opened his door to peer down onto the pilot to check if he was still holding on and to ensure that his physical stamina could sustain him for the remainder of the journey home. To increase their chances of successfully bringing the pilot back to Israel, Captain H. lowered his Cobra's nose dramatically, allowing the pilot to secure his armpit and forearms around the base of the landing skids—but there was no chance that the pilot would fall. As he later told his debriefers, "It was hard to hold on, but it was certainly easier than falling into enemy hands."

Having survived all adversity, the Cobra carrying its precious cargo landed momentarily on a secluded spot near the Mediterranean coast in order to allow the pilot to straighten himself out and to sit atop the landing skids in an erect, bicycler fashion—which was hoped to be more secure. But moments later, after a hurried takeoff, the two Cobras were informed that an AEU helicopter was flying close behind and perhaps it would be best if *it* ferried the pilot for the last leg of the trip back to Israel.

The Cobras landed and dropped the pilot off near the shoreline, at a point where the Litani River spills into the Mediterranean. Not knowing that an AEU Bell-212 was about to pick him up, the perplexed flyer angrily signaled with his hand toward the lead Cobra, thinking he was being abandoned. Suddenly, bursts of unfriendly fire were directed toward the rendezvous point. In the light from explosions of 20 millimeter cannon and RPG-7 rockets landing short of their marks, the pilot saw the silhouette of the AEU's chopper and finally realized what was transpiring. Without wasting a breath, the beleaguered flyer climbed back onto the landing skids of Major A. and Captain H.'s Cobra, banged with his fist on the fuselage to signal he was

A diminutive, though highly capable and maneuverable, remote-piloted vehicle stands at its small base in northern Israel, awaiting its video-controlled *takeoff and recon mission over enemy territory.* IDF spokesman

ready, and, once again, held on for dear life. Before liftoff, Major A. had the chance to look the pilot over for the first time and realized that he wasn't just an anonymous comrade in the IAF, but his favorite instructor from the pressure cooker days at pilot's course. The urgency to bring him safely back to Israel intensified greatly!

After the failed attempts to consolidate the pilot's tenuous grip on their aircraft, Major A. and Captain H. decided to go directly to Rosh Hanikra—without any further delay. They flew 100 feet above the water line at 100 knots. The AEU's chopper followed close behind until the Israeli border was reached and the final and emotional landing achieved. After his feet touched Israeli soil, the remnants of the pilot's stamina were exhausted, and he dully collapsed. As he was taken to RAM'BAM military hospital in Haifa, he demanded to know the fate of his aerial teammate, the Phantom's navigator, and wondered if he too was rescued in a similarly spectacular operation.

The pilot's navigator, Captain Ron Arad, was captured alive by Shiite gunners and at the time of this book's writing, in 1991, was still held by *Hizbollah* somewhere in southern Lebanon or Iran. His status as a prisoner and that of two other Israeli soldiers kidnaped by *Hizbollah* gunners in 1986 prompted the Israel Defense Force (IDF) to stage a dramatic kidnaping of *Hizbollah*'s southern Lebanon commander, Sheikh Abdel Karim Obeid, by a force of heliborne commandos on July 28, 1989.

The Hollywood-type rescue of the pilot on November 16, 1986, was a primer of what the IAF is all about. An integral arm of TZAHAL (a Hebrew acronym for the Israel Defense Force)—forming a triumvirate with the Army and Navy—the IAF has always been surrounded by a spectacular aura. Maybe it is because of the exclusive, lengthy, and brutally competitive training involved to transform a mere mortal into a flyer. Perhaps it is because of the space-age technology required to keep such a mighty, intricate combination of men, women, and machines flying. But just maybe it is because of the sleek and dangerous beauty of the IAF's aircraft and the power and awesome potential they possess.

In Israel, service in the IAF is considered an honor, a rite of passage, and a measure of one's worth. Only the best are allowed to volunteer into the ranks of the HEYL HAVIR, "Air Force," and they are expected to perform as the best. By supersonic jet, Damascus is but 4 minutes away, Cairo 3 minutes away, and Amman 2 minutes away. As a result, the IAF is the only one of Israel's combat arms where absolutely no margin for error exists. Every run-through, exercise, and task must be carried out flawlessly. Any miscalculation, nonchalance, and lack of vigilance could mean the difference between victory and defeat in a theater of conflict where defeat translates into the death of the nation.

This unique and uncompromising pressure on the IAF makes it an elite fighting body capable of spectacular feats. The IAF has an amazing esprit de corps and familylike atmosphere, which few other combat organizations can boast. Because of Israel's embattled status, the IAF's outnumbered predicament, and its role as the vanguard in the nation's defense, the men and women behind the aircraft's controls, watchtowers, and maintenance depots resemble a modern version of the Royal Air Force (RAF) during the Battle of Britain. Air Force personnel are a cut above the regular Israeli soldier—more disciplined, more mature, and unflinching in their dedication. Like their RAF counterparts from the dark days of the forties, the IAF's airmen and airwomen have their own unique language and lifestyle, and they view their responsibilities and duties as a campaign of pure and moral survival—the might of righteousness against the dreaded forces of evil.

The intense national pressure placed on the shoulders of the IAF does have its negative effects, however. The IAF's harsh demand for discipline and perfection exacerbates the soldiers' sense of loneliness and insignificance amid all those multimillion-dollar machines and the huge and impersonal confines of an air base. Their efforts might be appreciated by superiors and pilots alike, but they are never as important, or dramatic, as the efforts of the flyers or, in fact, the aircraft they service.

The pilots, on the other hand, must always live with the threat of combat and with new and more capable young pilots continuously being graduated from pilot's course. After surviving the grueling elimination process of pilot's course and amid constant in-flight training and combat operations, the pilots must conduct a normal life within the framework of the IAF. Each air base is considered the front line, and in this combat setting the pilot is expected to raise a family in neat impersonal homes engulfed in the roar of jet aircraft engines.

A nation's survival, which depends on an *individual's* courage and skill, is a powerful motivating force, especially in a nation that has never known peace. That obligation and pressurized responsibility, as well as Israel's ability to produce young men and women capable of meeting those challenges, has allowed the IAF to accomplish its deeds of daring. These acts have ranged from destroying thousands of enemy aircraft to attacking targets in such geographically diverse locations as Cairo, Damascus, Baghdad, and Tunis. The meticulous skills of IAF personnel allowed the IDF to pull off its miraculous rescue of Israeli and Jewish hostages at Entebbe, over 3,000 miles from Israeli shores, in 1976. In 1982, the IAF's indigenous technological mastery allowed it to nullify Syria's virtually impregnable umbrella of Soviet-produced sur-

The prototype of the LAVI, 1986. Michael Giladi, IDF spokesman

15

face-to-air missile batteries in Lebanon's Beka'a Valley, turning them into useless markers of the battle-scarred landscape.

Few air forces the world over have had such an uninterrupted cycle of war as has the IAF. The IAF has faced—and defeated—aircraft from World War II vintage workhorses to Mach 2 superfighters. Its pilots have battled a literal united nations of enemies—flyers who, in dogfights, have spoken Arabic, Russian, and even Korean.

As a result of such adversity against overwhelming odds, *innovation* has had to become an IAF catchword. The IAF has modified existing bought-off-the-shelf weapons systems to achieve amazing results. For example, in the F-4E Phantom, an aging workhorse obtained from the United States in 1969, the IAF is reported to have made over 600 modifications. Some have been major and highly classified, involving electronics overhauling; others have been minor and ingenious, such as installing cockpit rearview mirrors for the navigator. Other top-secret IAF modifications to other

Following a successful sortie against Syrian SAM sites on the Golan Heights during the 1973 war, three Phantom pilots watch the next wave head out for action. BITON HEYL HAVIR

weapons systems have enabled an antiquated surface-to-air missile such as the American-made Hawk, a threat to medium-altitude aircraft, to down high-flying speedsters such as the MiG–25 Foxbat.

The IAF has also been innovative regarding indigenously produced items. Its experiences with the French Mirage IIIC led to the creation of the KFIR, "Lion's Cub," family of delta wing, canard aircraft in the seventies—used by the US Navy's TOPGUN School to simulate the agility and combat performance of the Soviet MiG–21— and the LAVI, "Young Lion," fighter, a plane eventually downed not by Syrian SAMs or Jordanian Mirages, but by Israeli budgetary constraints. The IAF has used the novel idea of a child's remote-controlled propeller-powered toy in developing the remote-piloted vehicles (RPVs) that have become the envy of many of the world's air forces. The pilotless drones afford the IAF the safest means of conducting reconnaissance forays, the most cost-effective means of compromising enemy electronic defenses and delivering payloads, and an immediate, real time means of gathering field intelligence. Most important, perhaps, the IAF's operational innovativeness has led to spectacular operations where both human and machine have been pushed beyond all limits, such as the June 1981 bombing of Iraq's nuclear reactor and the 1985 bombing of Palestine Liberation Organization (PLO) Headquarters in Tunis.

For a nation whose name has long been synonymous with pious teachings and looking toward the heavens for inspiration as well as the odd miracle here and there, looking into the heavens at the world's most capable and battle ready air force has been the deciding factor in its quest for national survival. The IAF has been considered Israel's most prized possession. Throughout the over forty years of Israeli independence and wars, it has been in a class by itself and has continuously demonstrated itself ready to meet any challenge. The IAF is the best of the best for the simple reason that it has to be. The "right stuff" just isn't good enough; the IAF must have the "best stuff." In its life and death struggle, second best just will not do.

Chapter 2

History: From Turboprop to Mach 2

It is almost inconceivable that an air force as powerful as the IAF, a fighting force with supersonic speed, heat-seeking hardware, and space-age simulators, had as humble a genesis as the HEYL HAVIR did indeed have.

The roots of today's IAF can be traced back to preindependence Israel's illegal and underground army known as the HAGANAH, "Defense," and its ad hoc aerial component known as the SHERUT AVIR, "Air Service." The SHERUT AVIR was formed on November 10, 1947, after the civilian "glider-flying" Palestine Flying Club could no longer hide its military intentions. It was never intended to be an air-superiority-type air force, like the RAF or the German Luftwaffe, simply because the HAGANAH never thought it would be able to obtain aircraft fast and strong enough to do more than supply isolated desert settlements and conduct the odd bombing or strafing runs. The first aircraft the SHERUT AVIR could muster were light transport craft, mainly RAF Austers, originally designed as trainers.

With a force of eleven aircraft, the SHERUT AVIR flew reconnaissance missions, delivered mail, and, with luck and boldness, bombed enemy targets in crude and inaccurate "grenade tossing" means reminiscent of World War I. All that changed on May 15, 1948, when Israel declared her independence and the combined armies of Egypt, Transjordan, Syria, Iraq, and Lebanon invaded the newly formed Jewish State. On that joyous, though ominous, day, warplanes from King Farouk's Royal Egyptian Air Force began bombing Tel Aviv. The SHERUT AVIR had no real response.

Yet the HAGANAH was busy remedying the situation. Its arms procurement agents traveled to the four corners of the earth, including South America and Czechoslovakia, to obtain World War II surplus military material, especially aircraft. Within days of the Egyptian bombing, C–46 Commandos and C–47 Dakotas surreptitiously acquired through chartered means in the United States began ferrying crated Avia S 199s—oddly enough, Czechoslovakian, bastardized copies of the late war Nazi Me 109G fighter—to eager Israeli hands. They were pressed into immediate service, and two weeks following the declaration of Israeli independence, on May 29, 1948, four Avia S 199s attacked an Egyptian armored column only 20 miles from the outskirts of Tel Aviv. A week later, a SHERUT AVIR S 199 scored its

A Czech Avia S. 199 fighter, the IAF's first capable warplane, prepares to take off to engage Egyptian bombers attacking Tel Aviv, in June 1948. IDF Archives

first dogfight kills, shooting down two Egyptian C-47 Dakotas coming in for their "daily" raid on Tel Aviv.

Although the military value of the SHERUT AVIR's operations was negligible, its actions nevertheless served a psychological notice to the Arabs, whose invincible and overwhelming self-confidence suffered a serious blow. The Jews had an air force, and the SHERUT AVIR was renamed the HEYL HAVIR, the Air Force of the IDF. "Squadrons" were organized along the lines of a *real* air force, even though only a handful of planes existed.

In the months to follow, the HEYL HAVIR obtained, through guile, deceit, and cash-and-carry purchases, dozens of aged and obsolete aircraft from World War II junk piles. These aircraft included Bristol Beaufighters, Submarine Spitfires, P-51 Mustangs, and even the monstrous B-17 Flying Fortress. This "Tower of Babel" of aircraft was handled by a "Tower of Babel" of flyers.

The HEYL HAVIR's first pilots were an adventurous assortment of indigenous Palestinian Jews who had flown with the RAF during World War II, as well as American, Canadian, and South African veterans of the Second World War who found a moral calling to help the Jewish State's fight for survival. They spent the better part of their days swilling gin and reminiscing about dogfights over North Africa, Sicily, and France. They had no common language among

The Czech-built copy of the infamous Luftwaffe ME. 109, the Avia S. 199, which the late Modi Allon, the commander of the IAF's first combat squadron, flew to down two Egyptian C–47 Dakotas on a bombing mission over Tel Aviv. Note two kill marks near cockpit.

themselves, few operational aircraft to fly, and only the romanticism of a biblical struggle—the plight of David versus Goliath—to support their endeavors. In many ways, their esprit de corps surpassed their aircraft performance—especially since by October 1948, on the eve of Israel's largest offensive of the war, they had only seventy-eight operational aircraft—and pilot skill. This enthusiasm allowed the HEYL HAVIR to conduct brazen aerial sorties that even included the bombing of Cairo, Damascus, and Amman. Sometimes innovation and imagination had to take precedence over conventional military procedure—such as when soda bottles were dropped on Egyptian armor formations from light aircraft to simulate the use of real bombs—but, it got the job done! The HEYL HAVIR played an integral part in helping the fledgling IDF beat back the invading Arab armies and in the counterattack that achieved the "defensible" frontiers, which stayed in place until June 1967.

The armistice agreement signed between Israel and the Arabs in 1949 led to the immediate removal of the dire threat to young Israel's existence. Its signing also led to the removal of the backbone of the young state's air force, as the foreign legion of volunteers headed home after a job well done. Without the experience and semblance of military discipline these pilots possessed, the HEYL HAVIR had to continue its

The P–51 Mustang, in IAF colors, as used during the 1956 Sinai Campaign. The wily Mustangs, forever endeared for slicing through telephone cables in Sinai, remains one of the most enigmatic aircraft ever to sport the IAF's blue Star of David.

19

development from scratch—from a position of weakness and the unknown rather than experience and cultivated talent.

On March 15, 1949, the HEYL HAVIR graduated its first four pilots from a unique pilot's course. It was the first—and last—IAF pilot's course where all the students graduated successfully, where the training was conducted in English, and where, for lack of fuel and airworthy planes, only 150 flying hours were included. It was a humble genesis for a homegrown air force, but two of its graduates would have anything but humble careers. One of the first "blue and white" pilots was Danny Shapira, who became the IAF's chief test pilot and tested everything from the Mirage IIIC, to the MiG-21 Fishbed, to the KFIR, and, in the winter of 1989, a MiG-23 Flogger. The other notable graduate was quiet-tempered flyer Mordechai "Motti" Hod, who was the first Israeli pilot to fly a jet combat aircraft and, eighteen years later, commanded the IAF in its most impressive victory ever—the 1967 Six Day War.

With the wheels set in motion to bring the young HEYL HAVIR into its primitive own, several stages of development had to be accomplished for it to establish an effective and capable organizational structure. First, the nondisciplined military environment that the foreign volunteers instituted had to be replaced by strict and unflinching adherence to military protocols and procedure. Second, aircraft and equipment had to be procured, standardized, and maintained by home-produced technicians and engineers. Severe budgetary restraints limited the IAF to Second World War surplus piston-engined fighters, such as the British Mosquitos and American P-51 Mustangs bought at bargain prices from Sweden.

In 1954, shortly after the age of the first jet fighter combat by MiG-15s and Sabres in the skies over Korea, the Egyptians received their first shipments of British Meteor jets and Soviet MiG-15s. The infant IAF, on the other hand, was still flying planes made of wood, held together by glue, rusty nails, and luck! Making the IAF's predicament more precarious was Israeli prime minister David Ben-Gurion, affectionately known as the Old Man. An infantry veteran of the Ottoman Turkish Army of World War I, Ben-Gurion was not the greatest believer in, or supporter of, military air power.

Perhaps the saving grace for the IAF in its first difficult years was its commanders. Its first two commanders, Aharon Remez and Shlomoh Shamir, were controversial and short-lived figures. Remez, a veteran of the RAF, wanted the IAF to become a separate and exclusive Israeli military element. He faced an uphill battle to improve the quality of the IAF, especially in the wake of the hard-driving, devil-may-care, soldier-of-fortune attitude that the foreign volunteers generously left behind. He lasted less than a year. Shamir, a naval man, was brought into the IAF solely for his organizational talents; he lasted only eight months.

Then came Maj. Gen. Haim Laskov, a master at logistics. The architect of the IDF's first officer's course and one-time commander of the elite 7th Armored Brigade, Laskov restructured the IAF along professional lines, establishing a professional cadre of officers and noncommissioned officers (NCOs) and demanding stan-

Having survived yet another day of combat sorties against Egyptian forces, Israeli Mustang pilots happily return to base. IDF Archives

dards for IAF pilots to adhere to. Laskov was slated for bigger and better things—he would be the IDF's fifth Chief of Staff—and was replaced in 1953 by a native-born Israeli who had flown a South African Air Force Spitfire during World War II in the skies over Greece, Italy, and France. His name was Dan Tolokovsky, and he expanded the responsibilities of the IAF to include ground support, aerial reconnaissance, and long-range combat operations. Tolokovsky got rid of all nonstandard equipment, made pilots wear uniforms, and even ordered airplane mechanics to perform dreaded military drill. Most important, he inaugurated the IAF into the jet age.

The first jet the IAF acquired was the British Meteor, in 1953; close relations between Israel and France helped bring the Dassault M.D. 450 Ouragan, in 1953, and the Dassault Mystere IV-A, in 1956, to IAF service. Nevertheless, the quantity of these top-line aircraft in IAF service was limited, and piston aircraft were still used throughout the IAF's Order of Battle. Exacerbating the IAF's quality aircraft dilemmas was the unwillingness of most Western nations to offer training facilities to Israeli pilots. As a result, the fledgling IAF was forced to build from the ground up and, borrowing from the much-used cliché, allow the cream of the nation to rise to the top.

In April 1956, IAF jets downed three Egyptian Air Force Vampire jets in dogfights in the Sinai skies. At last, the IAF's emphasis on quality, to make up for its severe quantitative gap, began to shine through as Israel searched for aerial superiority.

On October 31, 1956, the Middle East erupted in full-scale war for the second time in seven years, in the Sinai Campaign. Hours before war was to break out, sixteen P-51 Mustangs flew a few feet above the sandy wasteland of the Sinai Desert and used their propeller blades to slice through Egyptian telephone lines; all sixteen returned safely. The IAF's unusual aerial opening shot was soon followed by a flight of sixteen C-47 Dakotas ferrying a battalion of paratroopers deep into enemy territory for their date with destiny at the Mitla Pass. In a statement of Israel's unique and embattled status—

as well as the egalitarian atmosphere prevalent in the IAF—the lead C-47 dropping the red berets into Sinai was piloted by a woman.

During the brief Sinai Campaign, the IAF was deployed in the all-encompassing fashion envisioned by IAF commander Major General Tolokovsky: piston aircraft and jets strafed roads and bombed enemy positions; Piper Cubs transported senior officers and conducted long-range reconnaissance forays; and transport aircraft supplied the troops behind enemy lines. The final results were equally as impressive: in 1,846 combat sorties, the IAF downed nine Egyptian fighters in aerial combat and destroyed 308 tanks and vehicles in strafing runs. Only fifteen Israeli aircraft were lost. The success changed Israel's view of its air force forever.

Israel's victory in the 1956 war led to a brief period of overconfidence in IAF ranks, since Israeli pilots met feeble Egyptian aerial opposition and, in accordance with the then secret joint Anglo-French attack on Egypt, Israeli skies were defended by F-84 aircraft from the French Air Force's *33 Escardrille*. Nevertheless, Ouragans and Mysteres were a marked improvement from the dark days and primitive aircraft of the 1948

A Gloster Meteor, circa 1955, the IAF's first jet aircraft. IDF Archives

21

War of Independence, and soon, Sud.Aviation Vautour bombers, Dassault Super-Mystere B–2s and Poter Air CM–170 Fouga Magister jet trainers were also obtained. During Major General Tolokovsky's reign as IAF commanding officer, the principal battlefield doctrine of the IAF was established, especially the objective of first destroying the enemy's aircraft on the ground and then concentrating *all* aircraft in a ground-support role. Ever budget conscious, Israel was turning its air force into an artillery component as well!

In 1958, the quantum leap in the development of the IAF of today came about when Ezer Weizman assumed command of the HEYL HAVIR. A boisterous and colorful individual, Weizman was an RAF veteran who had considerable combat experience and military insight. Known as Mr. HEYL HAVIR, Weizman reshaped the IAF into a modern and effective combat organization by transforming it into an elite club, a task helped by the relative peace that followed the 1956 war. An Israeli blue blood if ever there was one—he was a descendant of Israel's founding father, Haim Weizman—Ezer Weizman ordered the selective conscription of the best young men Israel had for its chosen club of future pilots. He coined the phrase and recruitment program known as HATOVIM LETAYAS, "best for the pilots,"

which was meant to urge on the elite young men of the nation to volunteer into unique, adventurous, high-flying familylike surroundings. His "best for the pilots" campaign angered many traditionalists in the IDF who wished to maintain the egalitarian image of the armed forces as well as preserve the sensitivities of the tens of thousands of nonflying IAF personnel. Mr. HEYL HAVIR stood fast, however. He knew that Israel's military predicament demanded that it possess the world's best air force, and he knew that only its human element could achieve that goal.

Yet the true turning point in Weizman's meticulously inspired stage of the IAF's development came in 1962–63 when France agreed to sell the IAF the trim, delta wing, silver devil known as the Dassault Mirage IIIC. The IAF ordered seventy-two of these Mach 2 aircraft, but, in the dawning age of the air-to-air missile, requested that they all be equipped with 30 millimeter cannons. Not that the Israelis were abandoning the age of push-button warfare, but, as Weizman later commented, "In accordance with our doctrine of removing the enemy's aircraft from the combat equation, once you've destroyed the enemy aircraft on the ground, air-to-air missiles are of little use!"

The enemy's air forces were to be removed from the equation, and quickly. The Mirage was

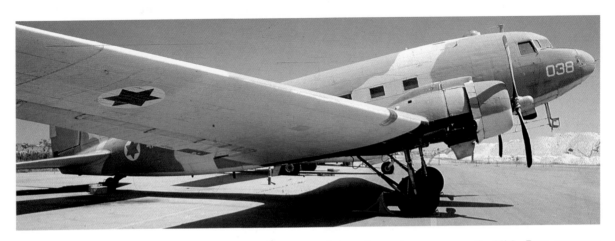

Strong and reliable, the Douglas DC–3 (C–47) Dakota is still flying in IAF service almost 30 years after it dropped paratroopers over the Mitla Pass. BITON HEYL HAVIR

22

soon pressed into service, and in a dramatic dogfight over the tranquil Sea of Galilee on July 14, 1966, a Mirage IIIC downed a Syrian Air Force MiG-21. It was the first downing by a Mirage, the first downing of a MiG-21, and the first IAF score in ten years. The year 1966 also marked the ascension to the IAF throne of a soft-spoken combat flyer who typified the "best for the pilots" maxim: Mordechai Hod.

Also in 1966, the IAF managed to gain something even more valuable than a top-of-the-line interceptor: an intimate look at the enemy's top-of-the-line interceptor. According to a foreign source, on August 16, 1966, in a Hollywood-type operation typical of the work perpetrated by the MOSSAD, Israel's foreign intelligence service, a young religiously persecuted Iraqi pilot was persuaded to defect to Israel along with his MiG-21. The aircraft, later given James Bond's infamous 007 designation, was carefully dissected by eager technicians, and its data was passed along to IAF pilots who soon became as intimate with the MiG-21 as with their own machines. That knowledge, an added edge, proved to be of monumental importance one year later in the IAF's most impressive display of prowess, might, and awe-inspiring guts.

On April 7, 1967, the Syrian Air Force and the IAF fought two concurrent dogfights over the contested border in the skies above the Sea of Galilee. The IAF's Mirages blasted six MiG-21s out of the sky to *no* Israeli losses.

In the weeks to follow, the precarious peace of the Middle East eroded quickly. Egyptian president Gamal Abdel Nasser ordered the United Nations (UN) peace-keeping force out of the demilitarized Sinai Desert—only to replace them with hundreds of thousands of Egyptian soldiers; Syria geared up for total war; and the professional British-trained Jordanian Army was placed under Egyptian control. In Cairo, Damascus, Amman, and Baghdad, jubilant calls to "push the *infidel* Jewish State into the sea" were heard over the airwaves, and in Tel Aviv, trenches were dug along the main streets, bomb shelters equipped with emergency supplies, and the reservists of the people's army mobilized. Israel, however, would strike first.

On the morning of June 5, 1967, as Egyptian combat pilots returned to their airfields following morning patrols and their replacements munched on hearty breakfasts, the IAF drew first blood. In a desperate gambit, almost every combat aircraft in the IAF inventory set out to destroy the Arab air power on the ground.

In less than three hours, hundreds of Egyptian planes were blasted to bits on their runways by accurate bursts of cannon and rocket fire. The IAF's attack was conducted in waves of aerial destruction. Special bombs known as PA'PA'MS (the Hebrew acronym for runway busters) were used to destroy the Egyptian airfields. The pride of the Egyptian Air Force—MiGs, Sukhois, Tupelovs, and Illyushins—never had a chance.

At the same time that the IAF's second wave was blasting a host of targets in Egypt, Syrian, Jordanian, and Iraqi air bases began to receive similar attention. Before the war on the ground began in earnest, Israel owned the Middle Eastern skies. In all, the IAF accounted for the destruction of 391 enemy planes on the ground, the total inactivation of sixty enemy airfields, and the downing of over sixty enemy aircraft in aerial combat. Once the Arab air forces were destroyed, the IAF dedicated itself to ground-support operations, mercilessly hitting retreating enemy tanks, vehicles, and formations. Fouga Magisters, aircraft designed as trainers, were pressed into service as fighter-bombers; armed with cannons and rockets, they were turned into effective though dangerous tank killers; Super-Mysteres dropped napalm on firmly entrenched Jordanian positions in the Old City of Jerusalem; and Mirage IIICs flew low-level strafing runs, destroying Egyptian convoys fleeing toward the Suez Canal.

During the six brief days of combat, not only had IAF pilots achieved gunnery scores that far surpassed their achievements in training, but the ground crews had attained a turnaround time between air sorties that left other air forces in open-mouthed awe—a feat that allowed the IAF to keep more aircraft airborne and fly more sorties than an air force its size could ever hope for. The IAF won the war for Israel; its relentless dedication and tireless efforts helped seize the Sinai Desert, the West Bank, Jerusalem, and the Golan Heights just as much as the paratroop reservists who took the Old City and the tank warriors who battled in the desert. The IAF had finally proven itself and displayed its destructive powers. Wars in the Middle East would never be the same.

Peace did not follow the 1967 war, and the IAF found itself more pressed than ever. Because Israel's preemptive strike sparked the conflict, the politically fickle French, the IAF's sole suppliers of combat aircraft, imposed an all-inclusive arms embargo and refused to deliver fifty much-anticipated and already paid for Dassault Mirage V fighter-bombers. President Nasser initiated a War of Attrition against Israel: a saturated conflict meant to use Egypt's vast numerical advantage in manpower and firepower to snipe away at Israel's resolve to fight and keep its newly captured territories. Israel responded with its traditional counter-measure: the IAF!

Along the Suez Canal, the Jordanian desert, and the Syrian hills, Arab artillery attacked Israeli positions and Palestinian guerrillas infiltrated into Israel; these actions were countered by Israeli special forces attacks on Arab positions. Operations performed by the IAF were the

vanguard of the Israeli effort and introduced two new players in the fray: the American A–4 Skyhawk and the F–4E Phantom.

The Skyhawk was a pugnacious little aircraft that was capable of 655 mph and could carry an ordnance payload in excess of 9,920 lb. With the Skyhawk, the IAF could drop an unprecedented tonnage of ordnance while deploying only few aircraft. The Phantom, on the other hand, was the aerodynamic definition of military superiority. A complete package of agility, speed, and strength—which made it a front-line interceptor as well as a fighter-bomber—the Phantom was capable of Mach 2.17 (1,432 mph) and could carry 3,020 lb of ordnance. It was the front-line aircraft of the US Air Force, Navy, and Marine Corps in Vietnam.

For years, American administrations were apprehensive about providing Israel with top-of-the-line military hardware, for both political and military reasons, a fear fatally justified with Israel's June 8, 1967, air and naval attack on the USS *Liberty*. The USS *Liberty*, a naval intelligence ship, was monitoring communications off the coast of Sinai. The Israelis believed it to be an Egyptian vessel.

The first Skyhawks reached Israel shortly after the 1967 war and the Phantoms in 1969. Both aircraft offered the IAF a new perspective,

The Iraqi MiG–21 that defected to Israel on August 16, 1966, painted in "war colors" and marked with its now familiar 007, sits aside a Syrian MiG–17 at the IAF Museum at HATZERIM.

added longer range, and carried heavier payloads. These pluses were coupled with America's friendly attitude to the training of foreign, especially Israeli, pilots—a welcomed relief from the IAF's somewhat stormy "marriage of convenience" with the French. Israeli pilots soon learned to appreciate that American planes were not only more sophisticated in their performance than French planes, but more reliable in the crunch and much simpler to operate in the heat of combat.

At about the same time as the first F–4E Phantoms reached the IAF in late 1969, Israeli paratroopers conducted an audacious commando operation. On the night of December 27, 1969, they landed on the Egyptian coast of the Red Sea at Ras Arab and attacked a surface-to-air radar base. Instead of destroying the installation, they hooked the top-secret Soviet-built radar to cables and whisked the monstrous device back to Israel by helicopter. The secrets uncovered by the dissection of the radar turned Egyptian ground defenses obsolete. That, together with the acquisition of the American aircraft, immediately changed the balance of power in Israel's favor. Soon, the entire nation of Egypt was in the bombsights of IAF craft, as sonic booms with Star of David signatures were heard over Cairo.

The IAF used almost every aircraft in its arsenal for the air war against Egypt. These operations sometimes consisted of dozens of aircraft—like the massive raid against Egyptian installations on January 7, 1970, known as Operation Bloom—or, as is often the case in war, lone campaigns of daring. On the night of October 24, 1969, for example, the IAF despatched two aging French-built Nord N.2501 Noratlas transports for a low-level bombing run against a Nile River bridge. Not surprisingly, the raid failed in miserable fashion and both aircraft were forced to return to base severely damaged. Such operations nevertheless expressed the IAF's all-out aerial effort against Egypt, as well as its feeling of ownership of the skies above Sinai and beyond.

But the Egyptians and Syrians had a trump card of their own: a powerful and generous ally called the Soviet Union. The Soviets carefully cultivated the Arab states with generous supplies of military hardware, including top-of-the-line surface-to-air missile (SAM) batteries, such as the SAM–2 Guideline and SAM–3 Goa, as well as hundreds of antiaircraft gun batteries, manned by over 15,000 Soviet officers and NCOs. The result: IAF deep-penetration raids against Egypt were met by murderous barrages of SAMs and accurate hails of radar-controlled antiaircraft fire. Soon, the IAF pilots began to suffer heavy casualties; aircraft were shot down in alarming numbers and dozens of pilots were killed in action or captured.

The Soviet-built and Soviet-manned missiles took a heavy toll on IAF aircraft and personnel, claiming the lives of some of the most successful Israeli pilots. One of those men was Phantom squadron leader Maj. Shmuel Chetz, who both Egyptian and Syrian MiG and Sukhoi pilots had learned to fear greatly. The cocky and balding Chetz had participated in some of the IAF's most audacious operations, including sorties against targets deep inside Egypt's Nile Delta and dogfights against Egypt's and Russia's best aces. He was killed on July 18, 1970, over the skies of Isma'iliya when a SAM–3 Goa ripped through his craft.

The War of Attrition culminated in explosive fashion on July 30, 1970, when a flight of fifteen Mirage IIICs and F–4E Phantoms ambushed a squadron of MiG–21Js flown by Soviet pilots. In the ensuing melee, which lasted all but 30 seconds, the IAF downed five of the MiGs without suffering a single loss. One victorious IAF pilot was a young Phantom skipper, Capt. Aviam Sela, who years later would be accused of "handling" the American spy Jonathan Jay Pollard.

The cessation of the War of Attrition did not end the bloodshed, nor did it end the uninterrupted operations of the IAF. Palestinian terrorist groups based in Syria and Lebanon frequently crossed the Israeli border to attack civilian settlements, often with horrendous results. Israeli policy regarding terrorism has always been one of immediate retaliation; terrorist bases and installations are decimated by commando raids and pinpoint aerial bombings following every act of terror. The sorties flown against Palestinian terrorist bases—usually located in the middle of densely populated refugee camps—proved an operational nightmare for the IAF. Because of the likelihood of hitting civilians, a direct violation of the IDF's policy of TOHAR HANESHEK, "purity of arms," the bombing runs had to be performed at low altitudes and in the face of barrages of intense antiaircraft small arms fire—as proved in Vietnam, a lethal threat to supersonic jet fighters.

The fanaticism of the terrorist war produced a disastrous incident. On February 24, 1973, days after various Palestinian groups vowed to crash a kamikaze plane into the heart of an Israeli city, IAF ground radar in Sinai picked up a Libyan Airlines jet heading toward Tel Aviv; IAF warplanes were immediately summoned for the interception. In midair, the IAF squadron commander ordered the Libyan aircraft's pilot to turn back, but he refused. With little time to waste, the decision was made and the airliner was destroyed by an air-to-air missile; all 108 passengers on board were killed. The downing of the jet was, however, a tragic accident. The Libyan jet had wandered into Israeli airspace after overshooting Cairo Airport, which was engulfed in a wicked desert sandstorm, and had refused the IAF squadron leader's urgent pleas to land at a nearby air base. For the IAF, 1973 had begun in telltale fashion.

Eight months later, on October 6, 1973, the State of Israel and the IAF were attacked again. Just hours before the Jewish State was to observe Yom Kippur, the holiest day in Judaism,

A smiling, upbeat, effective, and victorious IAF commander, Maj. Gen. Mordechai "Motti" Hod enjoys a moment of glory following the IAF's destruction of the Egyptian, Jordanian, and Syrian air forces and part of the Iraqi Air Force in 1967. IAF Archives

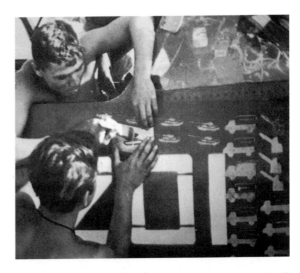

A Fouga Magister pilot has yet another enemy tank kill stenciled on his camouflaged fuselage after a sortie over retreating Egyptian armor in Sinai. Before the "tank killer" helicopter gunship, there was the Fouga. IDF Archives

Israeli Prime Minister Golda Meir—affectionately known as Israel's Iron Lady—received intelligence reports that both Syria and Egypt would be launching a massive attack against Israel later in the day. Realizing that a repeat preemptive aerial strike, identical to the one performed six years earlier to begin the 1967 war, would label Israel the aggressor and perhaps deny her valuable international political and military support, Prime Minister Meir opted not to act. With only conscript units manning the about-to-be-trounced-upon frontiers and hundreds of thousands of reservists being frantically pulled out of synagogue for Israel's fifth major war, 500 IAF combat aircraft, in bases from the Golan Heights to the Sinai Desert, were fueled, armed, and poised for action. Israel's hour was at hand, but this time, the nation would respond in desperation instead of initiating in rambunctious glory. It would be one of Israel's darkest hours.

The squadrons of Mirage IIICs, Phantoms, and Skyhawks were issued the difficult and dire task of keeping the Syrians and Egyptians at bay, to allow the reservists the time and opportunity to reach the front. The Arabs, however, had other plans. Incorporating lessons learned from the Soviets and the War of Attrition, the Syrians and Egyptians covered their division-size advances with mobile SAM umbrellas—consisting mainly of the SAM-6 Gainful; these missiles took an enormous toll on IAF aircraft, which had to fulfill an air-superiority as well as aerial-artillery role. The sophisticated Soviet SAMs accomplished what the Arab forces had never succeeded in doing: neutralizing the IAF.

Within the first few days of the fighting, while Syrian tanks reached within sight of the Sea of Galilee and Egyptian armor raced deep into Sinai, almost 100 Israeli aircraft were blown out of the sky. Most combat pilots flew exhaustive day-long sorties; flyers began their days attacking Egyptian T-62 tank formations pushing deep into Sinai and ended them 18 hours later bombing SAM-6 batteries near Damascus. Some pilots flew kamikaze-type sorties—flying

Armed with air-to-air missiles, the Skyhawk departs from its traditional role of attack craft for that of interceptor. BITON HEYL HAVIR

straight into SAM-2, SAM-3, SAM-4, SAM-6, and ZSU-23-4 quad-barrel radar-controlled 23 millimeter guns, engaging their radars while other aircraft attempted to destroy them. Nevertheless, during the initial stand-fast stage of the war, the IAF was able to provide much-needed ground support to the conscripts at the front, supplying absolute air cover to Israel proper while the reservists were mobilized and pressed into the struggle.

During the eighteen days of brutal combat, the hermetic Egyptian and Syrian SAM umbrella claimed 105 IAF aircraft. Most of these were front-line combat fighters, like the Phantom and Skyhawk, soon replaced by generous shipments from the United States in the "aerial bridge." The situation was so desperate that many of the American aircraft were borrowed from US units stationed nearby. The A-4 Skyhawks arrived at IAF air bases in their original US Navy Sixth Fleet schemes, and many F-4Es flown directly from West Germany arrived in Israel in their USAFE camouflage patterns and were sent to the front with a crudely painted IAF Star of David emblem to cover the stars and stripes. An American Phantom pilot who had flown dozens of sorties over North Vietnam and then settled in Israel found himself at the controls of the F-4E once again, engaging ground targets in northern Egypt.

The arrival of the replacement aircraft—forty-three Skyhawks and forty Phantoms—coupled with the ground campaign's turning in Israel's favor allowed the IAF to assume the offensive. With antiradiation ordnance received in the aerial bridge, according to foreign sources, IAF aircraft bombed and destroyed hundreds of SAM batteries while forcing the Arab aircraft into action. Over 360 Syrian and Egyptian aircraft were blasted out of the sky, and dozens of helicopters ferrying Syrian and Egyptian commandos were destroyed before they could deploy behind Israeli lines. The IAF aircraft bombed targets deep in enemy territory, including Egyptian air bases deep in the Nile Delta and the Syrian General Staff Headquarters in downtown Damascus. Although the IAF suffered an astounding casualty rate—almost twenty percent of its front-line aircraft and personnel—it was *the* difference between an Israeli defeat or victory in a difficult war that could have meant the destruction of the State of Israel.

Two important changes to IAF doctrine were proven effective in the bitterly fought 1973 Yom Kippur War: the multipurpose role of helicopters for rescue and elite force operations and the use of heavy transport aircraft to ferry troops and material to the front lines.

The IAF's first true contact with helicopters was in Algeria, in 1956, when a group of visiting IAF officers observed the French deploy them en masse against guerrilla forces.

In 1958, the first IAF helicopter squadron was formed, but its operational role was severely limited; in 1967, it mainly followed the advances of the ground forces and evacuated the wounded to hospitals back in Israel. In fact, before the 1973 war, the IAF made little use of its miniscule fleet of whirlybirds, made primarily of aging French Sud.Aviation SA-321-K Super Frelons and American S-58 Sikorskys, mainly because of their large size and vulnerability to ground fire. These aircraft were primarily reserved for vital transport roles, like ferrying a

A C-130 Hercules, the hero of the 1976 Entebbe rescue, takes off on a training mission. HANOCH GUTMAN, BAMACHANE

force of reconnaissance paratroopers to Beirut International Airport for a spectacular commando raid in December 1968 or providing an airborne taxi to infantry units pursuing Palestinian guerrillas in the desolate wilderness of the Jordan Valley.

When the IAF acquired the small and agile Bell-205 and Bell-212 Vietnam-era helicopters from the United States in the late sixties and attack helicopters in the seventies, Israel's use of the rotor-blades expanded dramatically.

The other change in the IAF's theory on its use of aircraft was also seen during the bitter battles of the Yom Kippur War when heavy transport aircraft, like the WWII-era Douglas C-47 Dakota and the newly acquired Lockheed C-130 Hercules, moved large amounts of essential combat supplies to the front lines in Sinai. Such aircraft extended the offensive range of the supply-hungry IDF and made the already confined Middle Eastern theater into a smaller place.

Three years later, on the night of July 3, 1976, the gigantic C-130 Hercules aircraft were immortalized when they flew 2,300 miles to shuttle a combined IDF commando force to Entebbe in Uganda and then bring the force back together with 103 former hostages rescued from the clutches of Palestinian terrorists. The raid, known as Operation Thunderball, warned terrorists worldwide to beware; the IAF would reach the four corners of the earth to protect its national security and the lives of its citizens.

Operation Thunderball was a brilliantly executed *land* operation, but it would not have been possible without the innovative minds in IAF Headquarters, the courageous men behind the controls of the C-130s, the fighter pilots who escorted the rescue armada as deep into enemy territory as their limited ranges would allow, the pilots of the IAF's flying ambulance who rushed the severely wounded to Israel, and the pilots of the specially fitted Boeing 707 command, control, and communication aircraft who supervised the commando forces on the ground. That aircraft, a combination of foreign and home-made electronic wizardry, witnessed the IAF's

entry into the Airborne Warning and Control System (AWACS) age.

In the years that followed, the IAF obtained the E-2C Hawkeye—an odd-looking propeller-driven aircraft with a rotating radar dish, which, when operating at an altitude of 30,000 feet, could detect aircraft 250 miles away, allowing technicians onboard to control several different combat situations simultaneously. For the IAF, an air force used to combat situations, it was a godsend.

The acquisition of the Hawkeye was part of an era that saw the IAF expand and diversify its aircraft from aging workhorses to top-of-the-line high-tech Mach 2 speedsters. Besides the production of its own advanced version of the Mirage IIIC—a canard and delta-wing fighter-bomber called the KFIR—the IAF obtained two high-tech masterpieces from America: the F-15 Eagle and the F-16 Falcon fighter-bomber. Whereas the KFIR provided the IAF with versatility and strategic depth, the F-15 and F-16 aug-

The newest addition to a successful decade-long legacy: the IAF F-16D. BITON HEYL HAVIR

mented the abilities and range of IAF operations.

This was best illustrated on June 7, 1981, when six F-15s and eight F-16s, piloted by, according to foreign sources, Arabic-speaking pilots, flew from the base in southern Israel across the Gulf of Eilat—then across the desert into Saudi Arabia, north toward Iraq, Baghdad, and Osirak: the nuclear reactor on the verge of producing weapons-grade plutonium. The reactor, deemed by Israel's leaders to be the greatest threat to Jewish existence since Auschwitz, was defended by scores of SAM-6 batteries and radar-controlled antiaircraft gun emplacements. The IAF flyers swooped in from the south and in one bombing dive turned the facility into a blazing inferno. They reached the target and returned undetected and unhindered by enemy radar, SAMs, and aircraft. The raid illustrated to the unconvinced the IAF's ability to accomplish the impossible and captured the world's imagination. In retrospect, with the Iraqi Scud missile attacks against Israel during Desert Storm, it might also have saved the world from a preview of nuclear Armageddon.

One year later, in June 1982, the IAF was in the midst of revolutionary transformations. Egypt, Israel's principal nemesis for over thirty years, was now a neighbor, not an enemy; peaceful relations had been secured by the Camp David Accords. The 41,000 square miles of the Sinai Desert, referred to by many as the IAF's testing grounds, was returned to Egyptian rule. The Phantoms, KFIRS, F-15s, and F-16s were all forced to train in restricted spaces, in high-tech

IAF pilots must always be prepared to fly and fight in the face of nuclear, biological and chemical (NBC) *attack. Here, two pilots in NBC kit return from their F-15s. IAF Magazine*

simulators, over the Mediterranean, and, in a harbinger of things to come, over Lebanon—where, since 1978, they had conducted retaliatory raids against Palestinian terrorist targets. It was here that the KFIR, the F–15, and the F–16 recorded their first kills ever: MiG–21s, MiG–23s, and MiG–25s that failed to evade IAF heat-seeking missiles and 20 millimeter cannons.

That full-scale war broke out in Lebanon came as no surprise. Terrorists from the Palestinian ministate in southern Lebanon and intense Syrian military activity brought intolerable threats to Israel's northern frontier. In the spring of 1981, Syria had deployed mobile SAM batteries in eastern Lebanon's Beka'a Valley, a move meant to hinder the IAF's bombing attacks against Palestinian factions allied with Damascus. Israel promised to remove the SAMs in a surgical strike, but US negotiations defused the volatile situation. When Palestinian terrorists critically wounded Israel's ambassador to Great Britain on June 3, 1982, chances for negotiations and peace were exhausted. The following day, IAF Phantoms bombed terrorist targets throughout Lebanon, including PLO Headquarters in the heart of Beirut; the Palestinians responded with massive Katyusha rocket attacks against Galilee. War was imminent.

On June 6, 1982, tens of thousands of Israeli soldiers burst across the Lebanese frontier, in Operation Peace for Galilee. The IDF—commanded by Chief of Staff Lt. Gen. Rafael "Raful" Eitan, an ex-paratrooper officer and certified jet fighter pilot, and the IAF commander, Maj. Gen. David Ivry—were determined to once and for all remove the Palestinians from Lebanon, and air power was to play a vital role. But the presence of over thirty Syrian SAM batteries in eastern Lebanon severely hindered IAF operations; this was a situation clearly not to be tolerated for long.

Between June 9 and June 10, in less than 48 hours, the IAF took out the Syrian SAM umbrella and most of the Syrian Air Force in an impressive and technologically masterful victory. Several IAF electronic intelligence aircraft were despatched to locate the missile site radars. Israeli- and American-produced remote-piloted vehicles, small propeller-driven "toy aircraft" equipped with advanced electronics and, some-

On October 11, 1989, Major Bassem of the Syrian Air Force defected to Israel in his MiG–23 Flogger-B. After undergoing a series of grueling tests in which it per- *formed opposite nearly all IAF fighters, the new IAF MiG–23 escorts an F–16 over the Old City of Jerusalem.* IAF Magazine

times, payloads were flown over the Beka'a Valley to act as decoys, causing the Syrians to turn their target acquisition radars on and engage them with their missiles—an operation that many have called Israel's Aerial Trojan Horse. With the electronic battlefield environment in its active peak, E-2C Hawkeyes directed squadrons of A-4, F-4, and KFIR fighter-bombers, all carrying antiradiation missiles and bombs, toward their targets. Destruction was complete and massive. In two days, the IAF destroyed over thirty once-thought-of-as-indestructible SAM batteries.

The Syrian Air Force responded with every plane they had. It sent in wave after wave of MiG-21 and MiG-23 fighters to intercept the IAF bombers, but they were met by awaiting squadrons of KFIRS, F-15s, and F-16s, all armed with Sparrow, Shafrir, and Python air-to-air missiles and guided by the E-2C Hawkeye. In the following three days of aerial combat, the IAF shot down more than sixty Syrian MiGs and Sukhois to *no* Israeli losses. During the three months of fighting, the IAF downed ninety-nine Syrian aircraft, including twenty by ground and antiaircraft fire; the only Israeli aircraft destroyed were a medevac helicopter, a Skyhawk, and an RF-4C reconnaissance Phantom—all shot down by ground fire or surface-to-air missiles. The virtual destruction of the Syrian Air Force allowed the IAF to concentrate on the true objective of Operation Peace for Galilee, and Palestinian targets throughout Lebanon were hammered daily by IAF bombing raids.

In the years following the 1982 war, the IAF continued its attacks against Palestinian and, later, Shiite terrorist targets in Lebanon and points beyond.

Budgetary restriction did not prevent the IAF from receiving a special and unexpected gift, however. On October 11, 1989, Maj. Mohammed Bassem of the Syrian Air Force defected to Israel along with his MiG-23—S Flogger-B, surrendering his Soviet-built fighter to a farmer at Megiddo. It wasn't the first Syrian aircraft to land in Israel—on August 12, 1968, two Syrian Air Force MiG-17s on a training flight mistook Haifa for Beirut and erroneously landed in northern Israel—but the intelligence bonanza to be gained by looking at the performance and electronic black-box defenses of the enemy's top-of-the-line interceptor was of great significance.

In January 1991, the IAF geared itself to fight yet another war—one which promised to make Israel's major cities the front lines. In the wake of Iraq's invasion of Kuwait and the subsequent Operation Desert Shield, Saddam Hussein vowed to burn half of Israel with his chemical weapon tipped Scud missiles should the allied coalition attack. Taking the Iraqi strongman's threats ever so seriously, much of the IDF and most of the IAF was placed on full battle alert. In fact, to reassure a frightened public, IAF commander Maj. Gen. Bun-Nun made a televised address in front of a fully armed F-16, its pilot ready in the cockpit to respond to any attack at a moment's notice. Although the Iraqis did, of course, follow through on their threats and Tel Aviv and Haifa were attacked by Scuds, IAF aircraft did not leave their hangars even though hundreds of the IAF's top of the line fighter aircraft—F-15s, F-16s, KFIRS, Phantoms and Skyhawks—were at the ready and poised for combat. Even though elaborate attacks against the missile sites in Western Iraq were planned, the United States urged Israel to sit tight and endure. It did, but, as will be seen later, Operation Desert Storm was a war in which the IAF became a full combatant.

The history of the IAF has been marked by over forty years of great struggle, sacrifice, dedication, and, most of all, uninterrupted combat. The IAF has achieved remarkable feats and incredible triumphs, being able to enlist the nation's most capable minds and bodies and training them to defeat all adversaries, be they Soviet or Arab pilots, and adversity, whether in combat over North African or in Levantine skies. Yet the IAF has had to pay a supreme price for its long list of impressive victories: 1,100 IAF personnel, mostly pilots, have been killed defending Israel's skies. Theirs is a dramatic story. But like the story of Israel's wars and the prospects for peace, it is a continuing saga that has yet to be fully written.

Chapter 3

The Best Stuff: The Pilots

The poster has been weathered by desert winds, rain, and years of preying eyes. On a chalk-white wall under the shade of an aged eucalyptus tree, the shiny image of four F-4E Phantoms—camouflaged, sleek, and flying in formation above the Old City of Jerusalem—is inspiring. Atop the photographed aircraft is the illustrated silver metal symbol of the HEYL HAVIR, the IAF. Underneath the Phantoms, and in bold type, are two words that strike a chord in the heart of nearly every Israeli male of military age: HATOVIM LETAYIS, "best for the pilots."

The assembled lot of young men who turned soldiers only moments ago appear nervous, frightened, and apprehensive. These new inductees in the IDF, gathered around a series of concrete huts, have a kitbag, a pair of shoulders and rear end heavy with harshly received inoculations, newly issued uncomfortable fatigues, and a dream. They all wish to be pilots—handsome and daring air warriors who will fly F-15s against Syrian MiG-29s, an F-16 driver who will gently place thousands of pounds of ordnance into the center of a terrorist training facility or a Syrian SAM battery near Damascus. Some have thought of hugging the earth in a Cobra attack helicopter, unleashing barrages of TOW missiles against enemy armor, and, in this age of Mach 2 speeds and air-launched missiles, a few just wish to be airborne and are ecstatic to be given the chance to fly the Hercules, or even a Piper Cub. But for most of these dreamers, being an air force pilot is nothing but a distant fantasy.

By the time an Israeli male hits the age of sixteen, thoughts of impending military service begin to occupy the mind. What will I do? Where will I serve? And, most prevalently, can I make it? Can I pass it?

It is GIBUSH TAYIS, or the weeding-out process that separates the young men who have the necessary physical attributes and intellectual faculties to become a combat flyer from those who simply do not. When an Israeli adolescent takes his first preliminary psychotechnical examinations at the IDF's Conscription and Absorption Base, his scores are immediately examined by Air Force personnel; those who are considered officer material and score well on their initial test will have their high school grades monitored and will be subjected to a further series of intense interviews and exams. KIBBUTZNIKS (members of KIBBUTZ, Israel's agricultural cooperative communities) are recruited most actively because of their keen acceptance of hard work, self-sacrifice, and ability to work within the framework of a team.

The pressure to do well on the long road to becoming a pilot is enormous. Being a pilot is *the* most prestigious thing to happen to a young Israeli. Forget being a successful businessman, forget politics. Being a member of the nation's most elite club is where it's at. For the hopefuls who fantasize about one day standing at attention at an air base and having the sleek silver and black cloth pilot's wings pinned to their chest, the fires of their visions have been stoked by years of conditioning: TV ads of KFIRS flying in formation and heroic accounts of pilots in the 1967, 1973, and Lebanon wars, which have become their history in the making.

Glory and history will have to wait, however. The airborne hopefuls are issued a 24 hour pass and ordered to report to an air base in central Israel at 0730 hours. The dream has begun.

GIBUSH TAYIS is, according to the thousands who have undergone it and failed, a week-long exercise of abuse, hell, and unimaginable degradation. For those who have passed, it is a tease: a harbinger of greater physical and psychological hardship to come. No matter how it is viewed, the purpose of the GIBUSH is to provide a pilot hopeful with a backbreaking, nerve-shattering welcome to the IAF. By forcing a recruit to suffer, march countless kilometers, perform guard duty, work kitchen duty, and cope with other pointless degradations, the Air Force hopes to determine the soldier's ability to perform under pressure; to adapt to adversity; to show initiative, leadership, will power, and quick-thinking qualities; and to perform within the framework of a team. Those who display anything less than perfect discipline, confidence, intelligence, and the odd hints of innovation are failed. Needless to say, most of the hopefuls in the GIBUSH will not see an airplane until they travel abroad following their military service.

The moment a recruit gets off the bus at the air base, he is greeted with the *nastiest* men the Air Force can find—pilot candidates in an advanced stage of their training—and are immediately ordered mercilessly around. "Stand at attention!" "Forward, jump!" "Backward, jump!" "Drop and give me fifty pushups!" "Thirty seconds . . . MOVE!" The tirades and abuse continue all day, until the hot Mediterranean sun gives way to dusk and the assembled men, already divided into platoons, have paraded through their temporary city of tents, carried all their gear piled on heavy iron cots to dozens of the countless hills surrounding the base in what's known as American Inspections, and have more than once questioned the sanity behind their choice for being a pilot. The GIBUSH commanders, wearing their neatly pressed khaki Class A uniforms, are only a year or so older than the poor souls they are torturing but well experienced in the rationale behind the cruelty. It's a task that is attended to seriously.

The soldiers in the GIBUSH feel lonely and confused. They all search out common acquaintances—friends from high school, friends of friends, and so on—and survive on rumors; they are, after all, only hours into military service.

In the first few days of the trial, the most feared words are, "In thirty seconds, head toward the water pipes and drink until you burst!" Drinking means physical hardship, and hardship means one of the two 18.6 mile forced marches that all the PRACHEI-TAYIS, "budding pilots," will have to pass: the first one is called the Preparatory March, and the second, and most difficult, the GIBUSH March. Stretchers are assembled for each march; each soldier is *expected* to help carry a comrade. The manner in which the soldiers conduct themselves in the 18.6 miles of steep hills and brutal mountainous terrain, as well as their ability to urge on their buddies and grab the jerry can and stretcher, are all noted by the ever aware, always-looking GIBUSH commanders. Nothing is unnoticed, and all information, from a soldier's physical stamina to his mental stature, is jotted down in small notebooks.

The last two days of the GIBUSH are when the hopefuls will sink or swim, when they're judged not by those on the road to getting their wings

For most future pilot hopefuls, this welcome to HATZERIM *Air Force base is too short-lived, because they'll be exiting the base, and the IAF, within a few days.*

but by actual pilots. For this process, all platoons are split into groups of ten, and each soldier has a large number drawn on his back and stomach in red chalk. As each MINYAN (in Hebrew, a prayer group of ten men) await their fate at attention, two figures suddenly appear. They are both pilots. One is a captain, in full Class A, with campaign ribbons, parachutist wings, and, of course, pilot's wings worn for all to see. The other, a first lieutenant, has his eyes completely covered by mirrored sunglasses and is dressed in his sage-green flight suit, which, together with his colorful squadron patch attached to the chest with Velcro, embodies confidence and unattainable ability. The pilots' presence leaves the hopefuls in awe, but unlike the GIBUSH commanders, the pilots treat the recruits with vague semblances of kindness. Kindness will not protect the hopefuls from the incoming insanity, however.

The two pilots escort their group of ten to an obstacle field. They present the ten with a 7 foot high wall and inform them that it is booby-trapped—electrified—and that they must cross it, carrying a metal barrel filled with imaginary explosives; what's more, they must cross it without touching it! Although the task appears impossible, a squad leader is chosen and they are given a few minutes to plan their undertaking and attempt to successfully execute it. As each try ends in failure, a new leader is chosen. Each pilot hopeful is given the chance to lead, and the pilots make lengthy notations as to each soldier's ability to command, to come up with innovative ideas and, most important, to face uncertainty and adversity.

Later, the hopefuls are also presented with mathematic equations they must solve verbally and offered pragmatic "real-life" situations they must solve with the certainty of a soldier, the compassion of a doctor, and the wisdom of Solomon. At the end of the two days, the frustrated group of ten is always offered a few words of encouragement and prepared for the next day's probable disappointment.

The GIBUSH TAYIS climax, known as Missile Inspection, is legendary in Israel. On the last day of the trial week, all the hopefuls, many limping, are ushered into a large auditorium where they will hear their future. The tension is supreme and, for many, too much to bear. Some mumble to themselves, others gaze hopelessly into space, still others pray that by day's end, they'll be issued with Air Force uniforms.

The air base's chief instructor enters the hall and is greeted by a hearty "ATTENTION," followed by a humbling "please be seated." In a monotone voice indicating that he has done this countless times, he says, "All those whose names I call please step outside." Nobody knows if those called are *in* or *out*; nervousness is replaced by anxiety and panic. As the commander reads out names according to the ALEPH, BET, and GIMELS— "ABCs"—the auditorium slowly empties, and finally, only dozens remain where hundreds sat only a short time ago.

As the alphabet comes to an end, those remaining become confident; but the roll call is resumed once again, and dozens more exit the room slowly and disillusioned. They will return to the Conscription and Absorption depot and

The much-dreaded "American Inspection" during the GIBUSH trial period of KOURS TAYIS. For a select few, this exercise in futility is the first step along their path toward the much-coveted pilot's wings. BITON HEYL HAVIR

35

will most likely volunteer for a GIBUSH to enter the naval commandos or paratroopers, forever wincing at the dream that died in that Air Force base auditorium.

After three read-throughs, the chief instructor gathers his clipboard and says, "All those remaining have passed the GIBUSH and will continue. Welcome to the Air Force." His departure is followed by hugs, shouts of joy, hearty handshakes, and, even in the machismo-dominated male world of the Middle East, kisses of relief. They've made it! They head on to the quartermaster for Air Force gear, have the tailor sew a white shiny stripe across the base of their newly issued gray-blue beret, and are even allowed to wear the silver metal Air Force badge with a white background, the rank and insignia of the PRACHEI-TAYIS!

Following the successful completion of the GIBUSH, the now-inaugurated budding pilots undergo a brief, two-week Air Force basic training, in which they learn the ins and outs of Air Force service as well as the correct manner of holding an unloaded weapon. The brief training concludes when the pilot hopefuls are marched to a landmark known as Mount of Pilots—a monument honoring the 1,100 Air Force personnel who have given the ultimate sacrifice—located in the hills near Jerusalem where, with one hand on a weapon and the other on a Bible, they will swear the oath of allegiance to the State of Israel as soldiers in the IDF.

If the IAF's grueling two-year pilot's course has one certainty, it is its uncertainty. Successful completion of the GIBUSH means nothing. At any point during the two years, from day 1 to almost hours before its completion, a budding pilot can be expelled from the course. In fact, nine out of ten fail, and the possibility of being washed out at any time inflicts a numbing pressure on all candidates—a pressure the IAF hopes will separate the best from the good and produce the material needed to fly an F-15 or an attack helicopter. The course is structured to allow the IAF to first examine a candidate's mental and basic airborne qualities; then concentrate on his physical and martial abilities; then focus on his ability to master a jet or helicopter; and, finally,

Still a long way from the F-15 and F-16 but an IAF aircraft nonetheless: the Piper Super-Cub.

look at his capabilities on a combat aircraft. The first step on this precarious path is known as HEKDAM, "Introductory."

Introductory lasts approximately three months—exact course times are considered classified—and consists of instruction in mathematics, physics, aeronautics, basic flight, meteorology, English, and, the culmination of much anticipation, ten training flights in a Piper Cub. Before these young men even learn how to fire a weapon, they are completing intensive studies and learning to fly. Before they are allowed to sit in the Piper, however, they must endure several difficult morale- and stamina-building marches—this is the army, after all—and, of course, exams.

The passing grade for a quiz and a routine exam is 65; the passing grade for important tests is 90 out of 100 . . . no exceptions! Those who continuously score below the passing grade—even if it's a few points—are ousted from the course, and those who have one or two bad tests are issued difficult make-ups and preempted from receiving the blue manual for the Piper, the most coveted aspect of the first phase of training.

Usually a course is divided into two groups: one completes its studies and then goes on to the Piper, the other receives its aerial baptism in the Piper and is then forced to study. Most wish to fly first, since they are at least guaranteed some air time before possibly being dropped from the course. Before they are allowed near the aircraft, however, a tension-filled 4 hour exam on the Piper's structure, flight procedures, squadron procedures, navigation, map reading, and emergency in-flight reactions must be overcome.

The Piper instructors are usually reservists or even civilian employees of the IAF, and each receives three pupils. At first, the experience is overwhelming. As a pupil enters the cockpit for his first in-flight lesson, the roars of combat jets flying overhead indicate a sense of power and might—something that is within the grasp of them all and yet so far from being attained. Wearing flight coveralls and actually speaking to the control tower over the radio spark brief visions of high-flying Mach 2 fantasies against enemy MiGs. The largest maneuver to be attempted with and without the instructor, however, is a humbling 60 degree turn with a 2.5 G-force.

To most pilot candidates, the first encounter with the G-force is unforgettable. As the force causes their weight to double, holding the throttle becomes difficult, as does regaining their composure to fly the aircraft—points all noted by the instructor. Some candidates have a hard time holding in their lunches in midair and, following a brief discussion with the course commander, are immediately dropped from the course, as are those who show indifference and little potential—the most popular phrase at the time being "promise you'll visit me in the Armored Corps."

At the end of the month of practice and functional learning, each candidate endures his flight test. Usually, a smile from the instructor indicates a favorable (passing) grade, but some, for reasons as miniscule as forgetting a postflight procedure, will fail and find employment elsewhere in the IDF. Already, after less than three months, the course has lost over half of its potential prospects through the KOURS TAYIS, "Pilot's Course," attrition.

Successful completion of Introductory is celebrated by jubilant cheers, and each candidate receives a plain navy-blue cardboard shoulder board as an honorary rank.

Phase 2 of KOURS TAYIS is known as MACHIN, "Preparatory," and is considered by many to be the most brutal element of the course—the one all pilots remember with greatest sentiment. It is here that the pilot candidates will finally learn to become combat soldiers.

Preparatory is, in essence, infantry school for pilots: a four- to five-month tour of backbreaking forced marches, weapons proficiency training, and, most important, survival exercises. But Preparatory is deceiving. In this stage, the candidates receive their new, *indoor* living quarters to replace their scout tents, and the comforts of an "urban" air base become pleasantly apparent. But their quarters are for sleeping, and that will be only on rare occasions.

As is now legendary in the IAF, the new members of Preparatory are introduced to their commander for the next half year just as they endear themselves to the luxuries of indoor accommodations. He is usually a lieutenant, a veteran of a reconnaissance unit, and cradles an assault rifle on a tattered sling. He is not an individual to be crossed. His first order is, "In thirty seconds, run towards the flagpole and run around until I say stop!" Preparatory is, after all, a pilot candidate's basic training.

After signing for a weapon, web gear, sleeping bag, digging tools, and all the other trappings of infantry training, the budding pilots, looking deflated in their olive fatigues, are divided into companies, platoons, and squads. For the next four months or so, their training will be identical to that which paratroopers undergo: a strict regimen of physical conditioning, weapons training, and combat courses. They are taught to handle every weapon to be found in the Middle

At the IAF flight school, an impressive row of TZUKIT aircraft—the Israel Aircraft Industries' rebuilt version of the French Poter Air CM-170 Fouga Magister dual-seat trainers—sit shielded from the desert sun in their open-air hangars.

East, from the standard Israeli-produced GALIL assault rifle to the Soviet AK series of 7.62 millimeter assault rifles and even the RPG-7 anti-tank rocket. A pilot shot down in enemy territory, for example, must know how to hold his ground and await rescue, in the process using any weapons found or captured. The candidates are also taught cold killing with knives and KRAV MAGA, the Israeli version of Oriental martial arts, which is a useful survival tool.

Unlike paratroop training, much of the physical training in the IAF's Infantry School does not emphasize reaching an enemy target but rather retreating toward friendly lines. The forced marches are brutal. They begin, recalling the GIBUSH, with a 18.6 mile hike, followed by more demanding distances and paces. Most candidates will pass out during one of Preparatory's 100 or so marches. The length of the training, and the conscription cycles, afford each soldier the ability to endure the torture in both brutal heat and shivering cold. Everything is done in a fast-paced march. The rifle range, for example, is 6.2 miles from their encampment, and each daily bit of shooting requires 12.4 miles of hell on foot. Some marches even last four days.

Perhaps the most important element of Preparatory is survival training. The companies of pilot candidates are taken to a field school where they are taught to save themselves from the enemy and the elements in nature; how to produce water in the wilderness—including covering certain desert plants with nylon bags and waiting for the water to flow; what to eat in the wilderness; camouflage; and how to escape and cover one's tracks. As the pilot hopefuls are considered valuable resources, their instructors are the best the IDF can find. Wilderness nutrition is taught by aged KIBBUTZNIKS who have spent their entire lives producing life from the desert; escape and evasion tactics are learned from Bedouin trackers, the most valuable asset to any IDF border unit and individuals whose inherent understanding of the desert allows them to read terrain with uncanny accuracy. Survival training takes the candidates from the snow-covered hills of the Golan Heights, to the wooded labyrinth of the Galilee, to the wasteland of the Negev and Arava deserts. Those who cannot handle the physical hardships are, in KOURS TAYIS tradition, dropped from the program.

Preparatory ends with a brutal graduation: a 74.4 mile march to be concluded in 24 hours, or less. Motivation in the ranks is always high, and what the body cannot do, adrenaline and pure will power take over. With the exception of those who break limbs, almost all candidates complete the march on two legs, or in some cases, on all fours. Following the march, the candidates receive a thin white stripe of achievement—and rank—for their shoulder boards. They are now considered infantrymen fourth class, a helpful degree of sorts should they eventually be expelled from the course and end up in an infantry or armor unit.

Preparatory is followed by a brief, month-long exercise in exclusion known affectionately as Check Eight—the process by which the Air Force will make its first determination if a pilot candidate should advance toward combat craft or helicopters, or serve as a navigator. In a brief ceremony welcoming everyone to Check Eight, candidates receive the much-revered pilot's battle dress jacket, a special mess hall, and, most important, the flight manual for the Fouga Magister training jet, affectionately called the TZUKIT, "Boulder," for its longevity, tenacity, and perseverance.

The TZUKIT is the IAI-overhauled, electronically advanced version of the French-built Poter CM-170 Fouga Magister dual-seat attack craft and trainer that first flew in 1956. In 1967, the Fougas were pressed into a ground-attack role, specializing in destroying enemy vehicles in low-level death-defying strafing runs. The aircraft—many adorned with so many stencils of known tank, truck, and jeep kills that their camouflage coats were covered—were also known as death-traps. Because they conducted their attacks from low altitudes, sometimes at tree-line levels, the Fougas attracted intense and accurate ground fire, and over a dozen were shot down. Because the planes were not equipped with functional ejection seats, many pilots tragically died in their cockpits. Today, however, these

Fougas have shed their camouflage covers for sleek white and red designs. They primarily serve as the showpieces for the IAF's aerobatic team and as KOURS TAYIS's introduction to jets.

The pilot candidates must master the theoretics of the TZUKIT within a pressure-filled three-week period. As is always the case in KOURS TAYIS, failing an exam means one make-up and, possibly, expulsion from the course. Exams are given almost daily now—testing that results in sleepless nights, extraordinary comradeship, and study halls filled with clouds of cigarette smoke. Although the candidates must excel in their studies for a spot in the course, they all realize that after the studies comes fly time. And fly time in the jet, capable of 433 mph speeds and tremendous G-forces, is, after all, the reason for the past year's grueling mental and physical torture.

The first flight with an instructor in the TZUKIT is an unforgettable experience. Many candidates are impressed at just being able to wear a flight suit and pilot's helmet. As they revel in their gear, the most feared man in their life—the TZUKIT squadron commander—enters the room, followed by a legion of instructors. The squadron

Two cadets in the Primary stage of training exchange some gossip and flying tips before a few more air hours in the TZUKIT. BITON HEYL HAVIR

commander cuts the thick cloud of tension by introducing himself and acquainting himself with each pilot candidate in the room; each soldier must rise, tell the squadron leader which part of Israel he's from, and describe his impressions of the course until now. Occasionally, a joke adds a roar of laughter, but the congeniality is short-lived. Much work is to be done.

As almost a year has already been invested in the training of these budding pilots, the Air Force begins to treat them with a little more "tender loving care." Instructors are matched to their pupils by personality and ability. Patience and all-hour assistance are offered to every candidate.

After a basic introduction to the cockpit apparatus, the flights begin. The first one usually is brief and around the immediate region. Each flight increases in length and distance, as do maneuvers, navigating, and in-flight "military" procedures, such as radio transmissions. Yet the instructors are looking for much more than a candidate's ability to learn. Each instructor is trained to pinpoint certain talents and deficiencies in a candidate's mechanics, coordination,

and abilities—aspects that, together with all the information gathered on the candidate since the age of sixteen, are carefully examined, meticulously studied, and analyzed. That analysis will determine exactly what kind of pilot the candidate will be and might determine what type of aircraft the candidate will eventually fly—still a long way down the road. That information is then passed on to the training squadron's commander, who, in an anxious ceremony to some and a joyous one to others, passes the results to his men.

The end of Check Eight passes into Primary with a weeding-out selection reminiscent of the Missile Inspection of the GIBUSH, but this time the candidates have invested much more than a week toward achieving their high-flying objectives. One year of pain, intense study, and unflinching discipline has gone into the pilot's course. The greatest fear is, of course, expulsion. "How will I tell my father, my mother, *my girlfriend* that I have been washed out!" Soon, in an auditorium adorned with glossy black-and-white photographs of IAF aircraft past and present, candidates who have prayed to be at

Morning rush hour on the flight school runway. A tzukit *competes for its place on line with two Skyhawks.* BITON HEYL HAVIR

the controls of an F-15 suddenly endure panic attacks at the thought of flying a Piper or another craft. Some fear they'll be helicopter pilots, some know that one bad exam has secured their fate as navigators. All curiosity is answered when the boisterous "ATTENTION" is sounded and the colonel, the squadron leader, enters the room.

The always monotone voice of the squadron commander sounds particularly void of emotion as he states, "All those whose names are called will continue training in combat jets." Shouts of jubilation are heard and the clapping of hands on comrades' backs fills the large auditorium as they know they will continue studies in the TZUKIT.

The squadron commander continues, "All those whose names are called will begin training in helicopters." The sounds of happiness are more muted as those selected to be either pilots or navigators imagine what their first lesson on the Bell-206 will be like.

"All those whose names I call will begin training as navigators"; they'll learn the ALEPH, "A," to TAF, "Z," of navigating on a Beechcraft, but their calling receives only muffled applause.

And then comes silence. Finally, "All those whose names are called are, I'm sorry to say, expelled from the course . . . see the lieutenant at the door for where you go from here!" Many of those expelled will experience a sense of depression and anger, which will follow them for the remainder of their military careers—in Israel, service that continues in the reserves, sixty-two days per year, until a soldier reaches the peaceful age of fifty-five. They feel deprived and cheated, but they have no recourse. Only fond memories of what was and what might have been.

For those whose talents guarantee—for now, at least—continuance in the course, this is the true beginning of their training. Some head out to learn the helicopters in which they'll serve for the next few years—attack choppers or

A Skyhawk, reserved for the most-advanced pilot's course pupils, undergoes routine maintenance from the dedicated, motivated, and experienced squadron ground crews.

transports. Those selected as jet pilots and navigators return to the TZUKIT and the *check-solo:* the final flight with an instructor before the lone venture into the heavens, the solo.

Sen. M. Sgt. Shlomo Yifrach, the three-war-veteran mother, father, and schoolmaster to future pilots, inspects potential one-day combat flyers before a military parade. Beyond the arduous training, incessant studies, and need to excel, most pilot candidates consider Yifrach's stern expression to be their most difficult rite of passage. BAMACHANE

Check-solo is a short flight meant to instill confidence in a candidate and is usually followed by the instructor's question, "Do you think you're ready for the solo?" Affirmative responses are met by, "So do it!" The instructor leaves the cockpit and orders the control tower to guide the future pilot to takeoff position. A few minutes later, dozens of budding pilots await the return of their comrade, eager to inaugurate his success with the traditional IAF greeting: a dunking with a bucket of water! Primary ends with an all-encompassing exam on the TZUKIT.

After a brief and unassuming ceremony in which they formally end Primary with a second white stripe's being added to their shoulder board, the trainees are led to a bulletin board and a brief memo. In small typewritten letters, the names of those who have been dropped from jets but will continue in helicopters or as navigators are listed. Pilot's course is still far from over.

The next step is called Basic and includes the goodies of flight training, formation flying, navigation flights, night flights—all in the TZUKIT. Although flying in the routine T- and E-formations are mastered with the TZUKIT with little fanfare, the dusk flights are awe inspiring. For these young men, who have endured much adversity in order to finally sit behind the controls of a jet aircraft of the HEYL HAVIR, pausing to admire and cherish the beauty of an amber sky as day turns into night is a memory long held. Flights in Basic include high-altitude sky grabbers and tree-line huggers, meant more than anything else to increase the motivation of a candidate. As opposed to everything being seen in the typical airborne post card view, suddenly hills, trees, electrical posts, and people appear very close; the candidate imagines what it was like in 1967, over the desert mountains in Sinai, to perform a strafing run at 100 feet against Egyptian tanks, the tank commanders aiming incessant bursts of machine gun fire at them.

Basic continues with a number of navigation flights, in which the candidates are given target coordinates and ordered to reach them and return in the shortest aerial route. Before each navigation flight, a candidate must draw two maps: one for his own use and the other for the instructor. The maps include landmarks, coordinates, targets, directions, and estimated times in which the target and return landing will be accomplished. The maps must be folded in advance for midair use inside the confines of the cockpit. The instructor grades everything, from the clarity of a map to how a candidate fumbles with it while at the same time attempting to control the throttle.

The navigation flights are difficult and are where most of those who will eventually be expelled from the course fail. For candidates used to an instructor guiding the way, being the lone soul at the controls for a flight to the unknown is a nerve-shattering experience. Those who perform with moderate success are reviewed and told what's needed to correct their errors for the future. Those who do poorly are invited to a private meeting with the squadron leader. Unlike the dreaded Missile Inspections, the conversation is meant to instill confidence and determine the reasons for weakness. Usually, the meeting ends with a pat on the back and the return of the candidate's self-confidence.

Soon, nighttime navigation flights, usually along the Mediterranean coastline, are conducted. Flights are difficult enough, but at night, the exercise exacts a demanding toll on a candidate's recently acquired abilities and leaves no room for error. The candidate finds himself in total darkness, relying on his map and successful reading of his instruments to guide him along the correct path. Soon, however, the bright lights of bustling Tel Aviv are seen. The air base and success are only moments away.

Basic concludes with a huge final examination, which, if passed, certifies a candidate as a TZUKIT pilot and is basically the candidate's last contact with the TZUKIT—unless he returns years later as an instructor or as a member of the IAF's aerobatic team. For those who fail the exam, a second and final chance is offered. Those who fail a second time are ordered to gather their gear and to find employment elsewhere. After Basic, each combat flyer will head toward study in the Skyhawk; helicopter pilot and navigator candidates will head toward advanced training

on the Bell-206; and navigators will learn in the C-47 and the Arava light transport craft.

Although the candidates have been placed, their destiny is still in their hands, as candidates have been expelled late in the course—even days before receiving their wings. The pilot candidates began the course over a year and a half ago along with hundreds of others, but now only a few remain. Will they finish it, or become an expulsion statistic—a story of failure that others will hear of in later courses? Nevertheless, each candidate participates in the beret burning ceremony, in which each soldier sets fire to his beret while being issued with the new, impressive black-rimmed officer's peaked cap.

As the popular saying goes, "After Basic, there is Senior Basic," and Senior Basic is the officer's course of pilot's course. For four months, the pilot candidates leave the addictive ambiance of jet engines and in-flight training and learn the art of command—IAF style. Dur-

Their boots shined to a mirrored sparkle, their commissioned officer's Class A uniforms ironed to perfection, soon-to-be pilots stand at ease; they await the moment when almost two years of labor and a lifetime of dreams will materialize with pilot's wings on their chest. BITON HEYL HAVIR

ing this period, they are called officer cadets and are issued with the final KOURS TAYIS rank of one thick and one thin white stripe worn on the blue cardboard shoulder board. The cadets are instructed in command and administration and in the history and structure of the IAF as well as the Arab air forces. They are also taught the secrets of enemy aircraft by men who have shot down MiG-21s, MiG-23s, and even MiG-25s. These men explain the technical insight behind the Soviet aircraft as well as the fighter doctrine taught in pilot's courses in Syria, Jordan, Iraq, and even Egypt.

Although it has been said of the Israeli pilot that his confidence and callousness are one in the same, he is taught in a mind-penetrating fashion that he is no better than his Arab counterparts. Overconfidence leads to underestimation, which, in turn, leads to tragic incidents in battle—especially at 30,000 feet in the skies over Beirut! Accordingly, Israeli pilots are taught to fight enemy pilots, *not* enemy aircraft. Of enemy pilots, they are taught to expect only the best, and they must respect the abilities and dedication of their opponents. Luckily, however, the IAF has shot down and captured enough Arab pilots so that many of their training secrets are now in KOURS TAYIS instruction manuals.

Senior Basic also means parachutist training. For the next three weeks, the candidates learn how to jump out of transport aircraft such as the C-130 or C-47. Parachutist training is considered an honor in the IDF almost to the point of being a rite of passage. But it offers future pilots insight as to what it might be like to eject from an aircraft suffering a malfunction or worse, decimated by an enemy SAM. After four jumps, including one at night, the candidates earn the right to wear the much-coveted silver metal parachutist wings. As they all expect to be pilots, they pin their wings above the right breast pocket, securing a spot on the left side for the silver and black cloth wings with the Star of David in the center.

Also during Senior Basic, the officer cadets undergo additional weapons training, as well as "operational assignments"—combat duty. They may serve along the Purple Line on the Lebanese border or against the Molotov cocktails and knives in the *Intifadah*, the Palestinian uprising on the West Bank and in Gaza. Even though the IAF has already invested countless hours and funds in their training, these officer cadets are, after all, soldiers and must serve where needed.

At the conclusion of Senior Basic, a cadet is "anointed" with an officer qualification badge and is given a single silver bar, indicating the rank of second lieutenant, covered by a piece of white tape. The cadets' final act in Senior Basic is to head to a base in central Israel and act as torturers and cruel souls—commanding a platoon in *this* year's GIBUSH TAYIS. Recalling their own suffering at the hands of similarly sadistic Senior Basic members, they attend to this task with great passion.

The final stage of the lengthy and tumultuous journey to become a pilot is known as Advanced. In Advanced, a pilot candidate begins to learn the TACHLIS, "truth," of being a combat flyer. The candidate is welcomed to the A-4 Skyhawk and receives its flight manual. For those about to be helicopter pilots, Advanced is conducted on the Bell-212. Helicopter navigators continue with the Bell-206; combat navigators continue with the TZUKIT, eventually reaching the much-revered F-4E Phantom; and transport navigators learn the awesome C-130 Hercules. Most important, perhaps, the pilot candidate in Advanced is considered a pilot and part of a squadron and is expected to act like a pilot; instructors begin to notice "small" idiosyncracies that are typical of cocky pilots, such as speaking confidently over the radio and *yelling* at the ground controller.

Most of Advanced is indeed spent in the air. For the combat flyer, besides the art of bombing and ground support, with both duds and live ordnance, and air-to-air combat, where the capabilities of the air-to-air missile and 20 millimeter cannon are attended to fastidiously, the skill of flying combat formations must be mastered. The refining of a pilot's dogfighting or bombing skills will be achieved in the squadron, but, to be able to train with the big boys, the pilot must know the correct manner to fly in formation when engaged by scores of enemy fighters or when embarking on an air raid against enemy SAM batteries in the Beka'a Valley.

A candidate must also still encounter endless examinations. Besides theoretic tests in combat doctrines and aircraft strategy, he takes tests that include knowledge of the types and capabilities of weapons systems in the enemy arsenals. A passing grade is 90 out of 100; those who fail are not permitted to fly until they pass a make-up. Nobody wants to become a statistic. Even though at this point the candidates are considered officers and, even if expelled from pilot's course, will remain in the Air Force in one capacity or another, they have ventured too far into the depth of inner discipline and study to fail now. Morale is at a hypnotic level, as is the urge to succeed. And finally, as if the two years have been nothing at all, graduation is at hand.

It is called Wing Inspection, and it is one of the most awe-inspiring displays put on by the IDF, a military organization not known for its pomp and ceremony. The ritual for the graduates of the KOURS TAYIS is usually held in midsummer and on Air Force Day—an IDF holiday of sorts that celebrates the Air Force and its personnel.

On the sun-soaked tarmac at the colossal HATZERIM Air Force base, near Beersheba in the Negev Desert, hundreds of family members and close friends gather in impromptu rows of seats hoping to see, if only for a moment, *their* pilot. Across from them sit the honored officiators of the gala: the prime minister, the IDF Chief of Staff, various officers wearing high ranks, and Maj. Gen. Avihu Ben-Nun, the IAF's commander.

Although the Chief of Staff, Lt. Gen. Ehud Barak is a competent combat officer and commands the enormous conglomerate of people and material that make up the entire IDF, the Air Force commander is considered special. He was chosen among hundreds of others to lead the most valued element of Israel's defenses. But Major General Ben-Nun is soft-spoken and modest—a man whose personality perhaps does not fit his awesome command. A graduate of, among others, Auburn University, the US Air Force War College, and the Harvard Business School, Ben-Nun commanded a Mystere squad-

ron during the 1967 war and was one of the first Israeli pilots to learn the attributes of the F-4E and fly it into battle. His most illustrious exploit was driving a Phantom in the epic air battle against Soviet-piloted MiG-21Js over the Suez Canal in July 1970 and even scoring a kill. Though his combat experience and administrative responsibilities have offered him great rewards, no returns are greater than watching another class of pilots graduating. It is, after all, the best assurance that under his command, Israel will always maintain air superiority.

The ceremony begins with a show of flags; all of the IAF's squadron colors are marched out for display. They are followed by the ceremony's honor guard of pilot candidates from the Primary stage of training, dressed in neat khaki Class As, their bayonets atop their GALIL assault rifles shining brightly in the summer's sun. The cadets are at times overwhelmed by their presence in the ceremony. Although they have rehearsed their drill for weeks, being the opening act for the Air Force commander is a difficult task, especially since they might never make it as pilots. After the mandatory "Present arms,"

The IAF commander, Maj. Gen. Avihu Ben-Nun, salutes the new class of pilots at Israel's most-awe-inspiring military ceremony. BITON HEYL HAVIR

45

"Shoulder arms," and "At ease," the pilot's course's legendary senior master sergeant, Shlomoh Yifrach, the man responsible for keeping the pilot candidates in line, yells the immortal words, "Officers and graduates, assume your positions."

Even as his voice utters the last syllable of the order, the "left, right, left" of the now-to-be-winged pilots arrives. They wear the Air Force's unique Class A uniform reserved for ceremony—a turquoise blouse and dark blue trousers—and have had the white tape that covered the second lieutenant bars removed. They are already officers, and in moments they are to become certified IAF pilots; all eyes are glued to a table next to the VIP seating gallery where a few dozen pilot's wings sit on a black felt tray, waiting to be pinned one to each pilot's chest.

An IDF band plays the HATIKVAH, "Hope," the Israeli national anthem, for the assembled. Following speeches by the prime minister and the defense minister and the Chief of Staff, Major General Ben-Nun takes the podium. He discusses the budgetary constraints being placed on the IAF and warns that "if Israel wants to live as a nation, it needs the best air force, and the best air force requires a large budget, one that guarantees the training flight-hours the pilots need to be ready to meet any challenge." The speech strikes a positive chord among the graduates who realize that their commander will do all for them.

As the last speech ends, show time begins. Show time in the Air Force means a flyby. First comes an aerial flag salute: a flight of Bell–212 helicopters carrying the Israeli, IDF, and IAF flags. That is followed by two TZUKIT flybys: one by pilot candidates from KOURS TAYIS and the other a breathtaking display of high-flying razzle-dazzle courtesy of the IAF aerobatic team, each aircraft using a different color of smoke to blaze a trail. Their accurate flyover is followed by a show of accuracy of another sort. An IAI-modified Boeing 707, fitted with a television controlled refueling system, refuels three of the IAF's most awesome aircraft: the F–15, F–16, and F–4E Phantom. The roar of the four jets humbles the crowd, as does the next "act," a flight of F–16s performing low-level, eardrum-shattering bombing runs. The final display comes from the AH–1S Cobra and Hughes 500 Defender attack helicopters, which fire TOW missiles at targets far off on the runway. The explosive thuds of the missiles hitting their marks impress the crowd and leave them in awe.

The exit of the helicopters brings the much-awaited and long-worked-for award of the coveted wings. Each pilot marches in front of the VIPs, salutes, and presents himself to Major General Ben-Nun, who, with great satisfaction and pride, pins on the wings. Some pilots get the wings of the navigator, some are cited for excellence, and all are immersed in emotion and sheer relief. As the inspection is called to order and finally dismissed, a monstrous roar, capable of competing with the F–15 in decibels, erupts from the newly anointed pilots, their peaked officer caps fly upward toward the heavens. Amid the ecstatic shouts of "I'm finally a pilot, a combat flyer!" comes the realization of the enormous responsibility, risk, and pressure those wings represent.

Each new pilot is allowed a brief period to bask in his glory before embarking on advanced

Pilot's and navigator's wings stand at the ready.
BITON HEYL HAVIR

46

A moment of sheer joy, undaunted pride, and mind-bending relief: newly commissioned pilots keep to tradition and throw their peaked caps into the air.

After a brief period of peaceful celebrating, their incessant work as combat flyers commences. BITON HEYL HAVIR

study on the Skyhawk, Bell-212, or C-130 and then heading out toward his final destination: the aircraft in which he'll serve for the next few years. The IAF matches a pilot's skill, reflexes, intelligence, and even personality with the aircraft he'll eventually receive.

The completion of pilot's course, a monumental feat, is, however, just a beginning. The pilots have now entered the realm of IAF operation, incessant training and competition, combat operations against determined enemies, and the responsibility of being the first line of defense for the nation's survival. It is an incredible task to expect of a twenty year old. Welcome to the real world. Welcome to the best of the best!

After pilot's course, after the wings, and after the celebration comes training and more training— here, conducted by two NCOs. BITON HEYL HAVIR

Chapter 4

A World Within It's Own: The Air Base

It is 0645 hours on a cloudy, miserable day, at an Air Force base somewhere in southern Israel, which, like every air base in Israel, is the front line. The Star of David flag has yet to be raised at the morning inspection, and only the muffled sound of aircraft engines and poorly tuned transistor radios can be heard. Within moments, however, the peaceful amber skies of an autumn dawn are about to be shattered.

At 0647 hours, the sirens of impending doom begin to wail. It is reminiscent of a bad war movie, but the sounds and state of emergency are real. Within seconds, hundreds of sleepy-heads race out of their living quarters, weapons and gear all in hand. On the outer perimeter of the gigantic installation in the desert, the gates are sealed shut; guards stop all incoming and outgoing traffic.

Infantry units attached to the Air Force—mainly reservists—are guarding the base and deploy alongside their armored personnel carriers. They lock and load their weapons and assume defensive positions beside key emplacements along the heavily fortified fence that protects the base's aircraft, ordnance, and personnel from the outside world. They are told to expect the worst: an enemy air raid or a suicide terrorist attack. They are also told to expect a horrible scenario, an attack by enemy surface-to-surface missile armed with chemical warheads; each soldier pulls out a gas mask from a pouch worn on the upper left leg and attempts to remember the correct procedure for dealing with chemical contamination.

Batteries of 40 millimeter antiaircraft guns have their barrels uncovered and raised toward the heavens while Chaparral and HAWK surface-to-air missile batteries prepare their fire-

The space-age cockpit display of an IAF F-16—flying in formation in the skies above northern Israel. IAF Magazine.

control radars for immediate action. Redeye handheld SAMs are even brought out in case an enemy aircraft manages to break through the supposedly impregnable shield of aircraft and antiaircraft missiles hardware.

Dozens of pilots, men who have slept in their flight suits, anti-G-vests, torso harnesses, and boots, race frantically up a flight of stairs from their underground sleeping quarters to their aircraft. On a rack loaded with flight equipment, each pilot grabs a brightly painted flight helmet and sprints toward the concrete shelters and hangars that house their aircraft. Under the shadows of camouflaged netting, the pilots put on special Nuclear Biological Chemical (NBC) Warfare suits over their flight gear as they run toward their aircraft. Ground crews, technicians, and bomb loaders, all wearing their baggy NBC kit, have fueled, prepared, and armed each aircraft. The pilot's orders will be received in midair; the important thing is the immediate takeoff before enemy bombs hit the runway, before the terrorists fire their RPGs at the $40 million aircraft and before clouds of poison gas engulf the area.

In less than a minute after the first siren was sounded, the roar of jet engines overwhelms the bustling air base as aircraft after aircraft is

From his perch at the control tower of an air base in southern Israel, a first lieutenant guides in the morning's first landing. IAF Magazine

OK'd for takeoff by officers and conscripts in the control tower—all of whom have been well trained for this eventuality. Emergency vehicles, ambulances, and firetrucks race toward the tarmac and hope that their services will not be needed today. Just in case it's full-scale war, ground crews have already prepared the fuel, bombs, rockets, and missile for the aircraft that will fly the next wave.

The exercise will continue for the next few hours. Plane after plane takes off from the base; the aircraft's ability to operate under such affliction is as much a testament to the flyers as it is to the ground crews and technicians. While the aircraft enact bombing and strafing runs against enemy ground forces and provide an aerial pocket of invulnerability surrounding the air base, the personnel on the ground are subjected to repeated scenarios and responses.

First is a gas attack: an "enemy" SCUD-1 surface-to-surface missile (SSM) with a chemical warhead has landed in the center of the base, and yellow—NBC—smoke grenades are detonated throughout the facility. The ground crews hide under plastic protective ponchos while medics prepare inoculations and stretchers.

Next, "enemy" bombs and SSMs have made the airfields inoperable; tractors, trucks, and engineers from the construction battalion quickly turn craters into leveled runways and destroyed bunkers into functional positions. Trucks fitted with large fluorescent projectors are brought on toward the runway to illuminate the field, should smoke or nighttime suddenly propel the air base into inoperable darkness. Fire trucks extinguish infernos caused by ignited jet fuel and exploding ordnance, while medics rush to treat the severely wounded.

On one runway surrounded by rows of concealing cedars, at a remote corner of the base, a special crew prepares to encounter an F-16 with a Hydrozine emergency. *Hydrozine* is a gas a pilot releases if he has a malfunction in his hydraulics systems; the Hydrozine produces static electricity, which in turn allows the pilot to operate the landing gear and other controls to allow the pilot to land the plane. The one problem is that Hydrozine is highly toxic; both the pilot and the ground crew risk poisoning and death from exposure to it. The "Hydrozine crew," as they like to be referred to, is supported by two fire trucks and two ambulances. With the life of a pilot at stake, nothing is left to chance. The first act of the crew is to instruct the pilot to shut off his engine; this, at least, confirms that the pilot is still alive. The pilot, Major B., is then gingerly removed from the Falcon and administered a gas mask and immediate medical care. Less than 30 seconds later, Major B. has an intravenous (IV) tube "attached" to his left arm and is rushed to the hospital.

The sirens, indicating attack after attack, wail throughout the day until finally they are silenced after every wartime scenario has been acted out and the last all's clear siren has been sounded. It's been an eventful morning.

The base commander, Colonel A., informs his squadron and battalion commanders that the chaos of the exercise is over and orders them to bring the base back to normal. In the event of a real attack, intelligence and warning time are relayed from Air Force Headquarters in Tel Aviv,

The highly advanced, much cherished, and already battle-tested E-2C Hawkeye is guided toward its protective shelter following a successful flight somewhere over the Middle East. BITON HEYL HAVIR

from the infamous BOR, "Pit," underneath the KIRYA defense complex in Tel Aviv (the IAF's nerve center), to the various air bases and units in the field. Because of the proximity of Arab air bases to Israel, warning time is reduced to only minutes, if that much. As a result, the ability of all personnel in the air base—from the battle-experienced pilots sporting the rank of major to the newly conscripted radar operator—to function in a coordinated, unhesitating, and *effective* manner is crucial if the air base is to maintain its own defense while contributing to the IDF's defensive and offensive strategy.

On a rain-soaked tarmac at an air base in northern Israel, a Phantom awaits its next operational assignment. BITON HEYL HAVIR

After a careful review, Colonel A. will determine if all the different units executed their tasks efficiently and if the base can be considered in "good operational shape" for war. However, room for improvement *always* exists; the IAF is never content with success. As he pauses to light his tenth cigarette of the short day, Colonel A. telephones his wife, pauses, and hopes that the real thing never comes.

Preparedness is essential for an air base to function in wartime, even for the IAF—an air force not familiar with defeat or adversity. At 1354 hours on Yom Kippur day, October 6, 1973, two IAF bases in the Sinai Desert, Refidim and Ophir, received a surprising invitation to war. Squadrons of Egyptian Air Force MiG and Sukhoi fighter-bombers appeared over the desert hills and began unleashing incessant barrages of rockets, cannon fire, and runway-destroying bombs.

At Refidim Air Base, the ex-Egyptian air base at Bir Gifgafa captured intact in 1967, the damage inflicted was devastating. At Ophir, the IAF was luckier. Not only did AA fire keep the MiGs at bay, but a squadron of Phantoms was scrambled in sufficient time to defend the base's territorial skies and chase and shoot down seven of the Egyptian intruders. The destruction at Refidim, however, prevented the beleaguered and besieged IDF units from receiving invaluable and, perhaps, lifesaving ground support from the IAF in the first few hours of the war. Colonel A., a veteran of that campaign in Sinai and one of the Phantom pilots who shot down the Egyptian MiGs, realizes that the preparedness of the air base is as important as the skill of its pilots.

An IAF air base is an enigma of sorts. It is a front-line combat position for an air force, and it conducts almost daily combat operations—bombing runs against terrorist targets in Lebanon, reconnaissance flights over enemy positions, and other activities. It is also a rear position, where female conscript-soldiers basically administer the day-to-day activities of million-dollar aircraft, cocky and confident aces, and thousands of soldiers. It is also a repair and technical facility, where technicians fiddle and tinker with electronics and radars.

The IAF backs its aircraft and complicated systems with a sophisticated technical infrastructure capable of handling all maintenance and service challenges. The technicians for this infrastructure are a highly motivated lot who work long hours so that their training, innovative ideas, and gadgetry aptitude might make already masterful weapons and avionics systems even more effective. Their abilities and dedication breed confidence and casualness; no saluting occurs in day-to-day activities and wing commanders are on a first-name basis with their ground crews, as the pilots realize that being able to keep the intricate aircraft airborne is just as important as blasting MiGs out of the sky. The technicians are, on the whole, career soldiers who have opted to serve the IAF rather than enjoy lucrative jobs with El Al, Israel's national airline. As a result, the atmosphere in the IAF, and the air bases in particular, is professional. Of the 30,000 Israeli soldiers who, according to foreign reports, serve in the IAF, fewer than one third are conscripts.

IAF air bases are also self-sufficient minicities, with swimming pools, movie theaters, and, as far as the IDF goes, comfortable living quarters. In some air bases—like Sde Dov outside Tel Aviv, which mainly handles liaison, light transport aircraft, and helicopters—discipline and work conditions are average—average, that is, for the IAF. In other bases, where the roar of F-15 and F-16 engines is heard round the clock, discipline is harsh, tension is rigid, and leaves and free time are few and far between. In the IAF, discipline is much more than a word, it is a philosophy—a state of mind required in the day-to-day activities as well as in war.

To the flyers, the air base is also a home, a self-contained environment where the pilot both works and lives. Because of Israel's embattled military predicament, the pilots must live on call, by the telephone, 24 hours per day, seven days per week; they must produce careers as well as personal lives near their aircraft. Alongside the blurry evaporation of burning jet fuel and the rumble of supersonic aircraft

Underneath the protection of a camouflage netting, an F-15 pilot, his identity protected by the censor's pen, climbs aboard his ship at an air base in northern Israel. BITON HEYL HAVIR

53

takeoffs and landings are neat, well-kept homes with tidy little gardens; mothers tow small children, who, in turn, tow puppies and kittens. The pilots' families are oblivious to their surroundings because they have to be. "Where's Daddy?" "At the office." That office is an F-15 or a KFIR.

The unique world of the air base is a complex and integrated macrocosm, but it revolves around the aircraft and the pilots who fly them. According to foreign sources, the IAF's Order of Battle consists of over 600 aircraft, including fifty-one F-15A, B, C, and D Eagles; 128 F-4E and Phantom 2000s; sixty-three F-16A Falcons; 200 KFIR C-2s, TC-2s, and C-7s; forty Mirage IIICJs and BJs; fifty-one F-16Cs (a further batch of seventy-five F-16Cs and F-16Ds will be delivered in 1991); and 140 A-4H and N Skyhawks. These aircraft are supported by, among others, four E-2C Hawkeye advanced early warning AWACS aircraft, twenty-one C-130E and H Hercules transports, two KC130-H tankers, and twelve Boeing 707 ECM and tanker craft. It is an impressive force, matched only by the skill, motivation, and dedication of its pilots.

For the flyers, their post KOURS TAYIS careers are filled with continuous competition, pressure, and operational assignments. Whether or not a pilot will get to fly the F-15—the air-superiority masterpiece that every soldier entering pilot's course hopes to drive—the F-16, the Phantom, the KFIR, or the Skyhawk does not depend on personal preference. The IAF has determined—through psychotechnical examinations and pilot's course grades, as well as instructor comments—the flyer's overall ability and the aircraft that is most suited to those learned skills and natural talents. A maverick, one not unnerved by high speeds and the natural appetite for the chase, might be slated for the F-15 or the F-16. Those showing aptitudes for accuracy in flight might also head for the F-16, or a less-glamorous attack craft, such as the KFIR and Phantom.

The pilots know, however, that each aircraft has an invaluable role to play in the IAF's scheme of things. The Phantom, and the Phantom 2000 in particular, is likened to the Armored Corps of the IAF; the KFIR and Skyhawk are the Artillery Corps; and the F-15 and F-16 are its commando units. The selection process that places a pilot with an aircraft is a delicate one that treads on many egos and aspirations but, as has been evident since the air campaigns of the 1967 war, one that has served the IAF and the State of Israel brilliantly.

Once in the air, however, rank, age, and experience carry no privilege. The best pilot in the formation, the one with the sharpest reactions, greatest moves, and most confident maneuvers, is the one who the others, even ten-year veterans and aces, must follow and emulate. In a flight of four F-16s, for example, a young and cocky first lieutenant who displays excellence in the cockpit will be the formation's leader; his number 2 can be a twenty-year veteran with the rank of lieutenant colonel; the number 3, a captain; and the number 4, a major. The flyer with the best skills will give the orders, command the missions, and ensure that the others in his group fly to his standards.

This phenomenon exists in no other air force and perhaps explains the unique character of the IAF. A pilot must continuously prove that he is not only an expert in a technologically advanced machine but a warrior, with killer instincts, as well. This competition also ensures that each flyer never ceases to be intimidated; the memories of pilot's course and the probability of expulsion keep his concentration and dedication constantly centered on perfecting his skills, studying aircraft manuals and reports, and always proving to be one step above everyone else. According to an instructor at the US Navy's TOPGUN School, "Israel has no average pilots. The *intimidation factor* teaches them to be competitive and to think for themselves, to always rely on their own skills and courage."

This intimidation factor manufactures unique psychological pressures on the flyers and, in some cases, eccentric personalities. It also produces awesome results. From 1966 to 1991, IAF pilots shot down 631 enemy aircraft in aerial dogfights—thirteen in the clashes of 1966-67, sixty-six in the 1967 war, 120 in the 1967-70 War of Attrition, 335 during the 1973 Yom Kippur War, ten during the skirmishes over

Syria and Lebanon during the "prolonged peace" of 1973-82, and eighty-seven over the skies of Lebanon in 1982—to only sixteen IAF fighters and bombers downed by Arab fighter pilots. The IAF's top ace is a three-war veteran, Lieutenant Colonel (Reserves) G., whose skills and tenacity and seventeen confirmed kills have earned him a place in the record books.

Israeli pilots are not the only Air Force officers who record enemy kills, however. Colonel K., a flight controller at a base in central Israel, claims forty-three enemy kills. At one time, especially between the 1967 and 1973 wars, aircraft radars saw only 2 miles ahead and the responsibility for foreseeing and controlling an aerial dogfight fell with the flight controller located on the ground. Colonel K.'s resume is impressive: on May 21, 1969, three MiG–21s; on September 11, 1969, two MiG–21s; on April 2, 1969, two Sukhoi 7s; in October 1973, fifteen MiG–21s, three MiG–17s, and a Sukhoi 7; on July 29, 1981, a MiG–25; and so on. His most challenging and most fruitful assignment was controlling the attack on the Syrian SAM batteries in the Beka'a Valley in June 1982. In 1991, Colonel K. commanded a busy IAF air base, guiding the pilots and aircraft that he directed in combat in the day-to-day activities of maintaining the peace.

Few flyers and flight controllers are as beleaguered as squadron commanders—people with a cherished job many consider the most challenging in the world. The MEFAKED TAYESET, "squadron commander," is responsible for the lives of hundreds of highly trained men and for hundreds of millions of dollars worth of aircraft. He is at the office a good 12 to 16 hours per day and is expected to lead some of the finest and most competent men in the nation by example. He is as influential a military commander as can be found anywhere in the IDF—many pilots have been known to sign on additional years of service only because they wish to remain with their squadron leader—and must be an administrative genius as well as a fearless combatant.

A day in the life of Lieutenant Colonel G., a chain-smoking commander of an F-16 squadron, consists of exhaustive work: planning, operational assignments, briefings, debriefings, and, of course, flight time. The day begins very early in the morning in the Squadron Operations Room where the pilots have gathered for their morning briefing. The pilots all appear at ease and comfortable; they wear their flight suits adorned with blue and white field ranks and rub their eyes harshly, attempting to awake for yet another day in the squadron. The operations room, filled with the aroma of strong Turkish coffee and stale nicotine, is large and well lit and consists of school desks, a blackboard, a video setup, and dozens of well-marked maps.

G. begins to outline the squadron's itinerary for the day: some need-to-be-worked-on low-level ground-attack techniques. The pilots ask questions whenever something is unclear to them. According to G., "The older pilots and the reservists are more comfortable with questioning a maneuver or technique, but not the youngsters. They fear that questions are a sign of

The finishing touches are applied to an F-16 pilot by his trusted crew chief, before an operational flight at an air base in northern Israel. As an IAF pilot will continually say, "A squadron is only as good as its support crew!" BITON HEYL HAVIR

After another "job well-done," a Phantom is guided back to its protective shelter at a base in central Israel. BITON HEYL HAVIR

Two officers take a stroll past a neat row of protected Skyhawks, at their base in southern Israel. Samuel M. Katz

insecurity or lack of ability and tend to keep their interest, or misgivings, to themselves."

Maps are detailed, flight plans are examined, and a hearty "meet you up there" is followed by G.'s ordering every pilot to be careful. As squadron commander, G. is responsible for being a fighter as well as a den mother, ensuring that all aircraft and pilots are airworthy for the day's work. These, like all actions, he does from personal example. On one night after a brutal training routine, for example, G. removed himself from a routine night flight because he felt too exhausted to safely fly his ship.

Before joining his pilots on the tarmac, G. races toward his office for a brief look at the morning's mail. The day's telegrams, all marked Top Secret, are brought in by the squadron's operations secretaries, two conscripts named Sigalit and Ilana. They enter his office without knocking, but, then again, they've never knocked. A laid-back atmosphere exists in the

Danger—runway! A warning to drivers and pedestrians alike that Mach 2 warbirds use this stretch of asphalt as a launching pad. BITON HEYL HAVIR

Fully armed F–16s are eased through the pretakeoff check, just before an operational flight along Israel's northern border. BITON HEYL HAVIR

An IAF show of force. Eagles await their drivers and a mission, in a multimillion-dollar parking lot at an air base in central Israel. BITON HEYL HAVIR

Dressed in their white coveralls and orange vests, ground crew members well experienced and trained in takeoff procedure evacuate the runway before the afterburners and throttles launch a flight of Falcons toward the heavens. BITON HEYL HAVIR

squadron, and the respect displayed toward their commander is not reflected in salutes or formalities, but in their eagerness to be a valued part of the squadron. Although they work for the squadron and enjoy being around the pilots and aircraft, their loyalty and dedication toward G. are unflinching. No matter if he's returned from a briefing or a sortie over Lebanon, he always finds time for their problems and welfare. The squadron is, after all, much more than aircraft and pilots.

After meeting his F-16 drivers on the tarmac, G. puts on his white pilot's helmet and is gently squeezed into the cockpit of his Falcon by Master Sergeant Yossi, one of the squadron's chief technicians. G. utters the TFILAT HADERECH, the Jewish prayer for journeys, which is taped to his cockpit windshield and then heads for the takeoff position. One by one, the F-16s line up on the runway, by now engulfed in a blinding sunshine, and head for the brief training foray in the heavens. Twenty minutes later, the squadron returns home; each pilot taxiing on the runway offers a thumbs-up to the ground crews who greet their arrival. Moments later, all the pilots find themselves in the operations room for the second time in the morning as a video cassette of the flight is played.

Besides laughing at a joke that "perhaps the training flight tape tragically erased one of the pilot's favorite Swedish films," G. is quick to point out mistakes, missed opportunities, and maneuvers where improvements are required. Because the pilots are a sensitive bunch, G. is careful not to bruise any egos, especially among men who find themselves in incessant competi-

tion with one another. This is not a popularity contest, however, and frank criticism might allow a pilot to perform a difficult procedure successfully in combat, which, in turn, might save some lives in the squadron. G. is also open to criticism and review. As he lights the first cigarette of the day's second pack with a Zippo received from a USAF pilot, he listens while several of his men question his own in-flight decisions and provide some of their own ideas. The squadron meetings are open forums.

G.'s squadron will be airborne two more times this day. They will practice numerous maneuvers, which, they like to boast, only *their* F–16s can perform. At 2100 hours, G. will review

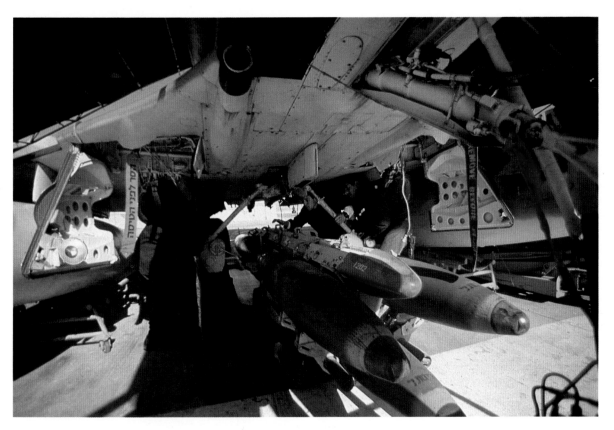

In a coordinated dance of agility and teamwork, a ground crew loads today's ordnance onto an awaiting A–4 Skyhawk. BITON HEYL HAVIR

his last file, put on his sage-green flight jacket, and head home to his wife and three children. "The only drawback with my position is the toll it takes on my family," says G. "Perhaps I'll take a year off, go to university, and be a civilian for a while. But, I'll be back. It's in my blood!"

Like G.'s F-16 squadron, each IAF squadron, from F-15s to KFIRS to attack helicopters, possesses a unique and somewhat religious type of pride—a following and dedication sometimes reminiscent of those exhibited by crazed sports fans. This pride not only hinges on the achievements of each squadron—which F-16 squadron was the first to score a MiG, which F-15 squadron bagged its first MiG-25, which one will kill its first MiG-29, and which KFIR squadron has the most accurate bombing scores—but on its histo-ry as well. The F-16 squadron commanded by Colonel Y., for example, is forty years old and has already gone through nine different types of aircraft and fought seven major wars. Looking at his aircraft and his pilots, however, Colonel Y. would not wish to go back in time—perhaps only to get the chance to wear a leather pilot's jacket and fly one of those precarious, propeller-driven World War II flying machines.

If the squadron commander, the experienced and wise group leader, is the heart of the squadron, then the pilots are its soul. Whereas the IDF is an integrated army, composed of all elements of Israeli society, a squadron is the integration of the IAF. The flyers vary greatly in age, experience, and temperament. Almost every day the combat flyers get some air time;

Armed with bombs and air-to-air missiles, a Phantom sits and waits for its ground crew after landing. The rearview mirrors attached to the cockpit are one *declassified Israeli modification made to the Phantom.* BITON HEYL HAVIR

Two C-130s sit idly by at their base in southern Israel. BAMACHANE

Its afterburners glowing, an F-15 takes off. BITON HEYL
HAVIR

the IAF flies more sorties per pilot than does any other air force in the world. Squadrons consist of men nearing the end of their military careers, flyers who have faced Egyptian MiGs, Syrian SAMs, and PLO ground fire, as well as new men—the cocky hotshots eager to prove their worth amid the sea of balding heads and experienced, highly tuned trigger fingers.

All pilots must perform daily; their actions, reactions, and performances are all reviewed and graded. The pilots realize that one small error, one lapse in a career filled with undivided concentration, might bring about an unfavorable comment from the squadron commander or, worse, a midair accident. They are taught from day 1 in uniform to compete and be the best.

The relationship among the pilots in the squadron is a difficult examination of psychological, sociological, and behavioral conflicts and bondings. The flyers are on the whole loners, men who solve their problems by soul-searching,

celebrate their victories alone, and endure the solitude and embarrassment of failure by internal chastising.

According to Lieutenant M., the pilot of a KFIR C-7 and a combat veteran, "The conflict which exists between the competition in the skies and that between the pilots on the ground is intense. You have to always try and be better than everyone else, but a pilot, no matter how talented, is a member of [a] team. We are all independents, 'pirates' basically, but we are a team. I'll beat him in the air one day, he'll beat me the next. But when we're flying a mission over Lebanon or should a big one erupt, we are all dependent on one another for survival. It takes a great deal of maturity and self-control to handle the competition in the air and the comradery on the ground." Lieutenant M. is all of twenty-two years old.

The one unifying element for all these pilots is their love for flying. They yearn for the chance to sit at the controls, to guide their ship through

A two-seat F-15B named Exploding Hand *stands ready for its green light and the exhilarating moment of takeoff.* BITON HEYL HAVIR

62

the takeoff, and then to match their well-honed skills against those of their mates in the squadron. The most favored bit of flying is the nighttime training mission.

Flying at night offers Lieutenant Colonel U., the commander of a squadron of F-16Cs, unique insight into the abilities and potential of his men and machines. A nighttime flight can be 70 minutes of space-age technology and peaceful black skies, with the cockpit lit up by the Head Up Display (HUD), radar lights, multicolored buttons, switches, and triggers.

Night flying tests a pilot's coordination, the ability to handle all of his instruments, weapons systems, and control by their illumination alone.

The pilots have to be "superawake," in a state of undaunted alertness. The danger exists that younger pilots might fall into a vertigo trap by not faithfully observing the radar, as does the danger that older and more-experienced pilots will use the darkness and the serenity to ponder questions of philosophy instead of studying their instrument panels.

It is 2030 hours at an air base in northern Israel. The bomb loaders, mechanics, and technicians have labored hours before the flight, loading bombs, fuel tanks, and SHAFRIR antiaircraft missiles. After the final preflight checks and adjustments have been made, the ground crews assist the pilots into their cockpits and

Three F–16s are photographed by an innovative soul through the cargo door of a C–130 Hercules, flying over southern Israel. IAF Magazine

head back to their quarters to watch the TV news—in Israel, a national and concerned habit.

On one runway of the F-16C squadron, four ships await the green-white lights of the runway and the takeoff signal from the control tower. The liquid crystal displays (LCDs) in the four cockpits serve as beacons on the darkened runway, but these multicolored silhouettes are soon racing on the tarmac, the grumbling of their taxiing replaced by roars of the 23,830 lb thrust Pratt and Whitney F-100-PW-200 engine. The takeoff is deafening but the sounds are sweet to the planes' mechanics, as is the smell of thousands of gallons of jet fuel evaporating into the air. In seconds, the aircraft head toward the stars. They are followed by another flight of four, and then another. Within moments, the entire squadron is airborne.

For five of the pilots, it is their first night-time training flight in the F-16C, and Lieutenant Colonel U. is a bit concerned. He makes a great

The IAF's Old Reliable: the F-4E Phantom. A veteran of the War of Attrition, the 1973 war, countless anti-terrorist operations, and the war in Lebanon, the Phantom embodies more power, might, and invincibility than any other aircraft in the IAF's arsenal.
BITON HEYL HAVIR

effort to see that they are comfortable with the exhilarating challenge of flying a machine like the F-16C in total darkness, but he is confident that pilot's course, studies on the F-16, and his own personalized guidance have prepared his young flyers well. Their mission this evening is to conduct a bombing run against a condensed cluster of "enemy positions." Every aspect of the flight will be scrutinized and examined at the postflight debriefing, and Lieutenant Colonel U. does not like to issue bad grades at night.

At a little after 2300 hours, the last aircraft has landed and all the red-eyed pilots head toward their favored seats in the Squadron Operations Room. The meeting will last several hours until Lieutenant Colonel U. utters the magic LAYLA TOV, "good night," and the pilots return to their quarters, peeling off layers of flight gear as they walk. The pilots all realize that they might never get a chance to rest and relax. With Israel's geographic-military situation being what it is, they might find themselves in the air in a matter of hours, only this time carrying live bombs instead of dummies and flying over Syria instead of over some KIBBUTZIM and empty hills in the Negev Desert.

Severe budgetary constraints mean that the flight time of the IAF's pilots has been reduced. As a result, the IAF's high-flying best of the best have had to settle for the next best thing: the simulator.

The simulator is a simple notion that makes up for the real thing with technology and a little make-believe. It consists of an exact replica of an aircraft cockpit, where the *trainee*—the generic term used for new pilots and graying reservists alike—sits as if he's behind the control of his ship and uses a set of mainframe computers that model all parameters of flight and reacts realistically to the trainee's adjustment of sticks and switches. The instructor plays the combined role of flight controller and the hostile elements: from changing meteorological conditions to an incoming cluster of Syrian MiG-29s. Hard copy printers record the training sequence. Most simulator trainers are female conscripts, soldiers barely out of their teens who sometimes guide the pilots through precarious scenarios that might have proved fatal in midair.

The IAF uses several flight simulators—the oldest and least-advanced being for the Phantom, the newest and most "Star Wars" being a model built for the F-16. Oddly enough, the most technologically deficient simulator, the one for the Phantom, is meant to duplicate the flight of one of the IAF's heaviest and most difficult to fly aircraft.

The twin cockpits of the Phantom trainer are firmly set on a moving mechanism of pistons, which enables it to roll, pitch, and yaw by 30 degrees in any direction. Because the cockpit is completely enclosed and blackened, the pilot must fly completely by instruments; at the time the training simulator was purchased, the technology wasn't available to reproduce the pilot's field of vision. According to Captain L., the commander of the Phantom simulator, "Flying the simulator doesn't at all feel like flying the real thing, rather it's like being inside a washing machine fitted with a video game."

The simulator cockpit cannot turn upside-down, nor can it accelerate at a high force and initiate Gs. The simulator does, however, allow certain indications as to the pilot's reactions and responses to the control of the engine,

Camouflaged perfectly to blend in with panoramic Galilee terrain, a KFIR *patrols the skies of northern Israel.* BITON HEYL HAVIR

Two KFIRS are joined by a modified F–4 Phantom and an F–16 Falcon for a flight over the port city of Haifa.
BITON HEYL HAVIR

Two ageless wonders still hard at work: an IAF-modified Skyhawk lending a helping hand to a Phantom. Both aircraft are 20 year veterans of IAF service.
BITON HEYL HAVIR

rudder, and ailerons. Nevertheless, to determine his simulated flight position and status, the flyer must always keep his eyes on the HUD or the instrument panel.

The simulator for the Phantom is, in particular, a most-valued brush-up course before getting to the controls of the real thing. New pilots are sometimes a bit too green and nervous to totally function behind the controls, and, with the Phantom in particular, many are reservists with long gaps between operational flights. They cannot remember everything, but any scenario, from a broken altimeter to a tailspin, can be fatal in midair.

According to one simulator operator, First Sergeant Mikki, the simulator saves lives. As the twenty year old sits behind the console of her computerized flying simulation contraption, proudly wearing her well-deserved pilot's jacket, a reservist pilot, who is also a father of five, enters the simulator cockpit to begin his predestined flight. After Mikki introduces several combat and aircraft system faults in rapid succession, the pilot gets entangled in an uncontrolled spin, his "aircraft" rotating violently toward "earth." Had that occurred in midair, the pilot might well have died and taken his navigator with him. But Mikki was able to talk the pilot through the chaos and bring him toward a leveled and uneventful landing. Although the flight was logged in the pilot's training record, it wasn't his last entry.

Whereas the Phantom trainer is elderly, the two simulators for the F–16, one for the A and B variants and one for the C version, are state of the art—the C model, heavily modified by IAF technicians, being the most fascinating. The cockpit is enclosed in a 24 foot diameter dome on which a full daylight scene is projected in an uninterrupted 360 degrees surrounding view forward, above, and on both sides. Unlike the Phantom simulator, the F–16 cockpit is specifically designed to duplicate the sensations of flight, including the onset of G-forces; a series of twenty-nine rubber cushions in the seat base, back, and sides are inflated and deflated in different patterns by air bellows—to experience *real* Gs, the pilots are sent overseas for a brief and unforgettable experience in a centrifuge.

The IAF takes "simulated reality" seriously, and many of the pilots entering their cockpits wear full NBC kit and flight gear and must check

The KURNAS–2000, *"Sledgehammer 2000": the IAF Phantom for the next century. This one faithfully carries Python air-to-air missiles.* BITON HEYL HAVIR

Making sure that her squadron's pilots have their equipment in tiptop shape, a young corporal examines a long line of flight helmets and G-suits. IAF Magazine

their weapons systems and arm their two AIM-9 air-to-air missiles—"one never knows when MiGs will be encountered during one of these flights," according to one trainee. All scores and performances, be they brilliant executions of well-taught maneuvers or tragic errors, are scrutinized, meticulously graded, and recalled on the next flight.

No matter how technology manages to copy the thrill of flight inside a computer-induced experience, nothing can copy the real thing, especially a combat sortie.

In April at an air base in central Israel, a Squadron Operations Room is crowded for the morning's routine briefing. Yet the room is filled with tension, anxiety, and fear, and nothing is routine about that. For the pilots of a Phantom 2000, known as the KURNAS, "Sledgehammer," squadron and a Skyhawk squadron, the regular "good mornings," cups of calming coffee, and joking around are replaced with deathly silence; thoughts of "what's for lunch in the mess hall" are replaced by obsessive thoughts of 14.5 millimeter and 23 millimeter antiaircraft guns and SAM-7 Strella handheld antiaircraft missiles. All eyes, belonging to both young and old pilots, are directed toward the Phantom squadron commander, Colonel Z., who will command both squadrons in today's operation.

Colonel Z. paces up and down by the blackboard, pointer in hand, and circles the area around the port city of Sidon, a labyrinth of Palestinian terrorist training camps hidden in the midst of refugee camps; it is as dangerous a target area as can exist. Today's specific target is a terrorist training facility belonging to, according to foreign reports, Abu Nidal's *Fatah* Revolutionary Council, located 5 kilometers northeast of the city. The operation's targets are circled by colored markers: the Phantom's targets in red and the Skyhawk's in blue.

For a space filled with warriors about to enter battle, the Squadron Operations Room is a pretty sterile environment. It is engulfed in a blinding white glow, mirrored by glossy white walls, yellow formica tables, and bright fluorescent lights. A 10 foot long, 3 foot high blackboard is loaded with dozens of sliding maps and intelligence photographs taped adjacent to chalk-written flight assignments. An identification chart is also taped near the blackboard, allowing the pilots to refresh their memories as to the exact silhouette of a MiG-27 Flogger and the flight pattern of Soviet SAMs. The pilots are told what their mission is and what to expect over the missile- and projectile-congested skies of Lebanon. Taped to the wall throughout the room are photocopied pages of the latest proclamation of the intelligence reports.

Colonel Z.'s instructions are meticulous, straightforward, and listened to religiously. "Remember this is a mountainous region; the target, five kilometers northeast of Sidon, is on the northern slope of [a] steep hill, an area familiar to you all from previous operations. The view is very pretty, almost like Switzerland; . . . from the attack altitude, you'll be able to see the snow-capped peaks of the Lebanon mountain range in the north. Intelligence reports a concentration of terrorists due south of the target—east of Buqasta, near Sidon. Due north of the target are Syrian Army roadblocks, adjacent to Lebanese Army positions. Near those positions are clusters of Druze villages hemmed in by other terrorist positions. In a corridor between the Awali River and Beirut, there are additional Syrian Army positions—with, of course, their complement of AA hardware. As all ships will be taking off at close intervals, *bombs must be released in the minimum of time spans!* You'll go in tight, and remember, accurate releases. Accurate releases, I repeat, *accurate releases.* As always, be on the guard against antiaircraft fire, missiles, and cannons. Whoever sees a launch coming towards his direction informs the other ships and immediately engages the sources of enemy fire. Always engage the sources of enemy fire before dealing with your original target."

As Colonel Z. will lead the attack, the other pilots synchronize their watches to his: "Three, two, one, press. Synchronization!"

Sitting silently on the side is Brigadier General R., the base commander. After Colonel Z. ends his talk, the base commander, a charismatic figure, begins his pep talk to the pilots. "This operation is definitely limited to what you've all executed successfully in training. This is *not* total war, however. I want absolute professionalism. Every bomb—on the target. I want a small 'click' of the bomb-release button, a boom, and then get your asses the hell out of there. This operation demands absolute identification of the target; . . . release your ordnance *only* after the target has been absolutely identified. We don't want to kill any innocent civilians or damage any civilian property . . . and there are many civilians near your targets. Please be careful, come home in one piece, and good luck!"

Before dismissing his men, Colonel Z. reiterates that the most important element of this operation is teamwork, between pilot and navigator and between the different aircraft. The pilots then head to fetch their gear, making sure all their survival gear is in absolute working order; the commando knife is examined and placed confidently back into its scabbard, the Beretta 9 millimeter automatic is checked, and the handheld signaling device receives one last battery check.

In the khaki-gray army bus that ferries the pilots to their aircraft is absolute silence. The

An officer supervises nighttime landings and take-offs from the control tower at an air base in central Israel. BITON HEYL HAVIR

tension, adrenaline, and thoughts of mortality begin to absorb the bus; the reservist driver attempts to break the ice by putting on the radio, but the sounds of the blues are not improving the temperament of the flyers. The radio is ordered extinguished seconds later. All the Phantoms and Skyhawks are lined up in neat rows. The ground crews, technicians, and bomb loaders, their light blue work clothes already covered in grease and sweat, have prepared each aircraft with its fuel, external fuel tanks, 20 millimeter ammunition, and bombs; sights are calibrated to perfection, hydraulic systems examined, and ECM systems checked. For an operational flight, every system is checked, doubled-checked, and even tripled-checked; the crew chiefs must sign out every aircraft, guaranteeing that a ship's mechanical, hydraulic, and weapons systems are ready for combat.

The ground crews help the pilots into their cockpits, fasten their belts to the ejection seats, and adjust their shiny red flight helmets to perfection. One by one, the aircraft taxi toward the

One generation of fighter pilots brings the possible next generation to see a most remarkable craft: the F–16. BAMACHANE

runway and takeoff position; Brigadier General R. follows this progression in a white Ford Escort staff car, which is dwarfed by the sleek and delta-winged aircraft camouflaged in shades of sand, green, and brown. The roar of the engines appears to almost blast away the runway lights, and the force of the vibration rattles the bombs and fuel tanks hanging underneath; the pilots prove impervious to the noise and motions. The "last chance man," the technician on the tarmac who gives a final examination to each aircraft before takeoff, issues a thumbs-up to the pilots after ensuring that everything is all right and ready for Lebanon. The ships line up for takeoff position. The control tower gives its authorization, the flaps open, and the afterburners are ignited.

This process is repeated a dozen or so times until the last aircraft disappears into the brilliant blue sky. Although raids against Lebanon

At a central location near the main runway, emergency services vehicles stand at the ready—just in case.

have already become "routine" for the IAF, all of the squadrons' officers are nervously gathered in the base's nerve center. Each officer in the room has a friend in the sky, but there is nothing to do but to hurry up and wait.

The increased clattering and hissing symphony of radio communications indicates that the aircraft are nearing their target. The first ship to dive onto the target and hails of small arms fire and trails from two Strella launches is Colonel Z.'s; he unleashes his bombs, and the explosions' thuds are followed by dozens of other bombs and the rattling of 20 millimeter cannon fire. Within minutes, a thick cloud of gray smoke engulfs the mountain, and the aircraft begin their egress. Because of the proximity of Lebanon to Israel, the formation of Phantoms and Skyhawks reaches the Mediterranean shore at Netanya—a resort town situated halfway between Tel Aviv and Haifa—in minutes and heads back to base.

At his debriefing, Colonel Z. tells Brigadier General R., "The field targets, strewn about a series of buildings, were dealt with *effectively* in the attack. Vehicles found near the compound were also destroyed. Some of our younger flyers have now earned membership in the 'operational club,' and they, in fact, performed quite admirably. We also surprised them completely. Each Phantom and Skyhawk flew in perfect attack formation, identified its targets, released its ordnance, and then raced towards the sea. Everything went according to plan and was BESEDER, 'OK'!"

The next day, the IDF Spokesman's Office releases a brief statement on the raid, informing the press that "our pilots reported accurate hits of their targets in southern Lebanon, and all of our aircraft returned safely to their bases."

Anonymous, unheralded, and with little fanfare, the pilots of the squadrons return to their day-to-day routines of training, operations, and more training. Graduating pilot's course, after all, was never meant to secure one's glory or celebrity status. The men in the cockpits of the Phantoms, Skyhawks, KFIRS, F-15s, and F-16s do it because, if Israel is to survive, *someone* has to. And that someone, fate and hard work have determined, is them.

Chapter 5

Blue and White Whirlybirds:
The Helicopters

September 15, 1987—the area known as *Fatahland* near stoic Mount Dov, in southern Lebanon. A force of infantrymen from the IDF's elite GIVA'ATI Infantry Brigade on an afternoon's patrol 7 kilometers inside the 12 kilometer wide security zone, the mapped-out frontier that separates Israel from the terror inside Lebanon, had fallen prey to the worst scenario any infantry formation can succumb to: the ambush. A force of over fifteen Palestinian ter-

Two Bell–212 choppers, the true workhorse choppers in the IAF's arsenal, pass the peaceful and tranquil *snowy abyss near Mount Hermon during a routine patrol.* BITON HEYL HAVIR

rorists, armed to the teeth with AK-47 assault rifles, RPGs, and mortars, had surrounded the company-size force with an inescapable ring of fire. When the setting sun shined brightly in the eyes of the Israeli force, the terrorists placed the GIVA'ATI officers in the middle of the cross hairs of their Soviet-produced weapons and opened fire. The company commander, a platoon commander, and a squad's 7.62 millimeter FN MAG light machine gunner were cut down instantly in the first deadly volley. Their deaths, as well as

Links in the chain of every tank soldier's worst nightmare: AH-1S Cobras, flying in a formation of tank-destructive firepower over the rolling hills of northern Galilee. BITON HEYL HAVIR

the barren mountain terrain and impending darkness, made the GIVA'ATI force's predicament extremely precarious; time and options were both running out. With the cries of the wounded and the clamor of automatic fire making radio communications difficult, the distress signal was sounded and the IAF's cavalry was summoned.

Seconds after the first call of an ambush was received, a Bell-212 transport chopper, the IDF's aerial taxicab, touched off from its base in northern Israel with reinforcements. The chopper had been on alert from the onset of the GIVA'ATI patrol, but the emergency signals from the security zone initiated a frantic response procedure. The pilots studied their maps quickly and fastened their sight-helmets and mirrored visors; the door gunners cocked their FN MAGs; the ships were fueled; and the infantrymen, armed and mentally prepared for combat, raced toward their helicopter—its rotor blades swinging around with increased velocity—for the short trip to the unknown. The Bell-212 flew at top speed and at treetop level, reaching Lebanon in just minutes. The transport and attack helicopter pilots who fly their sorties over southern Lebanon call it Little Vietnam, a reference to the sometimes impregnable hails of ground fire that greet the beating sounds of their rotors. They found no enemy fire, yet!

Darkness had already fallen, and the 212's number 2, First Lieutenant Z., made successful navigation to the ambush site possible by faithfully following his own markers and calculations on the map. As communication was established between the Bell-212 and the ambushed GIVA'ATI patrol, terrorist fire began slicing through the air; the bright green lines of tracer fire gained the attention of the pilots and the sheer panic of the helicopter's belly-load of infantrymen.

The 212 had two options. The first was to escape the hails of Palestinian fire and find a location somewhat removed from the heated exchange of lead and explosives to unload the reinforcements. The second was to make an immediate, dangerous, and highly volatile landing. Helicopter pilots are also—though sometimes overlooked—the best of the best, and they seldom settle for easy solutions. The pilots informed the door gunners that they'd be landing *right here and now* and that the services of their accurate eyes and tireless trigger fingers would be required.

As First Lieutenant A., the 212's skipper, brought his ship down in the middle of the battle, the doors of the chopper were slid open and the infantrymen cocked their GALIL assault rifles and prepared for the instantaneous exit they'd trained so relentlessly to achieve. First Lieutenant A. lifted hard on the throttle, gliding the 212 gently atop a huge boulder. The 212 received no cover from the ground; the GIVA'ATI infantrymen were engaged in the close-quarters battle with the terrorists, and the 212's door gunners raked the area below with incessant volleys of 7.62 millimeter machine gun fire. The moment the landing skids touched earth, the GIVA'ATI reinforcements raced out and assumed a defensive perimeter while First Lieutenant A. informed the GIVA'ATI commander on the scene that the cavalry had arrived but was "getting the hell out of there." The IAF, however, was not through for the day.

As the Bell-212 got its "target rich" silhouette out of Little Vietnam, two AH-1S Cobras, which escorted the 212 from a distance, made their much-valued appearance. At first, they hoped that the mere sight of a helicopter gunship, armed with multibarreled guns, TOW missiles, and 2.75 inch rockets, might deter the terrorists. It didn't. The terrorists were a determined, well-trained, and courageous group of men who were in it for the long haul; it was them or the GIVA'ATI infantrymen and they were resolute to gain a victory for Palestine or martyrdom.

The battleground was a labyrinth of hills, boulders, and *wadis*. Located 7,000 feet above sea level, it was exposed to autumn winds that were fierce and unforgiving, making even routine flying an eventful undertaking. The first Cobra attempted to engage the enemy from 500 feet, but it was dark and the combatants were fighting too close together to risk a rocket or round unless they were absolutely sure it would not harm the GIVA'ATI. Relying on the coordinates relayed from a beleaguered GIVA'ATI medic—who

by now had pretty much assumed the role of company commander, communications officer, and field doctor—First Lieutenant G., the number 1 Cobra pilot, lowered his nose and fired four flares; his gloved fingers gripped ever tighter on the throttle's trigger switch. He also glanced toward the 5.56 millimeter CAR-15 assault carbine loaded with two magazines taped together, placed near his leg. This was Lebanon, and one properly placed projectile, one lucky RPG shot, and "this baby goes down." The helicopter pilots flying low-altitude sorties must always know where their personal weapon is just in case they're forced to rough it. Otherwise, they're as good as dead or, worse, POWs.

From the northern flank, RPD machine gun fire from three different positions began to chase the Cobra. First Lieutenant G. fired several bursts from his 20 millimeter cannon at the terrorists; the volleys of shellfire softened the Palestinian's resolve, but it didn't destroy it. In fact, the only indication as to the accuracy of the

After keeping a force of ambushed GIVA'ATI *infantrymen alive with incessant firepower in September 1987, the pilot of a Cobra helicopter gunship, Captain Y., meets with IAF commanding officer Maj. Gen. Avihu Ben-Nun, left, and IDF Chief of Staff Lt. Gen. Dan Shomron to receive a well-deserved medal of valor.* IDF spokesman

75

IAF's fire was whether or not the bright muzzle blasts of the terrorists' fire were darkened—permanently. The GIVA'ATI force attempted to regroup time after time, but they were met by murderous hails of automatic fire and had to be guided in battle by the overall view of the Cobra pilots. To direct the fierce fire-fight, the Cobra had to fly at the dangerous hovering altitude of only 100 feet.

The battle continued for the next 12 hours. The Cobras refueled and rearmed numerous times, and a third GIVA'ATI reinforcement squad

Hard at work, a Cobra mechanic endures the brutal summer's sun for some much-needed work on his ship's engine. BITON HEYL HAVIR

was ferried in by First Lieutenant A.'s Bell–212. Saving the GIVA'ATI patrol was dependent on exact coordination between the attack choppers, the Bell–212, and the accurate trigger fingers of the chopper pilots. Whenever a terrorist or the muzzle flash from his RPD machine gun would be spotted, the Cobra pilots would dive in for the kill. They'd aim their 20 millimeter cannons and, according to First Lieutenant G., "Squeeze the trigger until 150 to 200 shells would disintegrate the terrorist position in an instant." First Lieutenant G. continued: "One terrorist, who attempted to engage me head-on, found himself buried in an explosion of shrapnel fragments and shredded boulders." By dawn's first light the next morning, the battle and the aerial marathon had ended. The skill and courage of the pilots had enabled a force of infantrymen to endure a dire and determined terrorist ambush.

Seven months later on Israel's fortieth Independence Day, the date when Medals of valor are usually awarded, *Captain* G. and *Captain* Y. were summoned to the office of their commander, Maj. Gen. Avihu Ben-Nun, and an audience with IDF Chief of Staff Lt. Gen. Dan Shomron. Captain G. was issued the TZA'LA'SH HA'RA'MAT'KAL, "Chief of Staff's Medal of Praise," for his courage under fire, and Captain Y. was given the TZA'LA'SH MEFAKED HEYL HAVIR, "Air Force Commander's Medal of Praise"; the previous year, the IAF handed out six such medals to helicopter pilots operating in the north.

As the two young pilots left their commander's office, they noticed three large glossy photographs. The first was of a McDonnell Douglas AH-64 Apache attack chopper displaying its 1,200 rounds of 30 millimeter shells, sixteen Hellfire laser-guided antitank missiles, and pods for 2.75 inch rockets. In March 1990 the IAF signed a contract with McDonnell Douglas for the acquisition of nineteen AH-64A Apaches; the first of these attack-choppers, the most advanced in the world, arrived in Israel months before the Gulf war broke out. The second was of a brilliant red and white Aerospatiale SA.365 *Dauphin,* "Dolphin," hovering over three IDF Navy missile boats. And the third, hanging near the Apache and the *Dauphin,* was a black-and-white of a Sikorsky S-55 transport, circa 1965, crudely camouflaged and flying over the then-divided city of Jerusalem. Captain Y. looked toward Major General Ben-Nun, smiled, and said, "We've certainly come a long way, haven't we!"

The IAF's helicopter corps has come a long way. The first whirlybirds to sport the IAF's blue and white Star of David emblem were two odd-looking American Hiller 360s, which the IAF acquired in March 1951, over the objections of David Ben-Gurion, who believed that the miniscule Israeli defense budget could better use its resources to purchase additional rifles and bullets or, if aircraft *had* to be obtained, fighters like the P-51 Mustang or bombers like the B-17 should be bought. Nevertheless, Ben-Gurion understood that many of Israel's independence war difficulties, such as the need to supply cutoff settlements and the inability to evacuate casualties, could have been solved by the helicopter. Duly, several pilots were removed from their beloved piston-engined fighters and given *9 minutes and 5 seconds* of instruction in the Hiller. A new generation had indeed dawned for the IAF.

Initially, the IAF did not fully comprehend and appreciate the versatility of the rotor-powered, peculiar-looking aircraft. The effective deployment of the helicopter in Korea, however, was a pronounced development on the battlefield that the IAF could not overlook. Israel's then close-knit military relationship with France afforded several IAF pilots the opportunity to visit French forces in the bitter battlefields in Algeria and imagine what the IAF would be able to do with these silly-looking contraptions.

Slowly, and with great skepticism, the IAF purchased several more helicopters. First came the Bell-47 and then the Sikorsky S-55. Although helicopters did not participate in the October-November 1956 Sinai Campaign, the IAF used an S-55 soon afterward to rescue a force of reconnaissance paratroopers who had wandered into an extensive Egyptian minefield in the Sinai Desert. A few weeks later, several S-55s were used in a covert mission deep inside Jordanian territory.

The IAF's bond with the whirlybird had begun, but little could anyone have realized that the amusing aircraft so useful for evacuating wounded and ferrying generals and cargo would one day kill tanks and hunt subs. Nevertheless, the IAF realized that the helicopter did indeed have potential and, from the onset, maintained firm control over the aircraft. Although helicopters would assist armored, infantry, and naval units, the IAF operates all helicopters used by the IDF.

His KIPAH *("skullcap"), squadron patch, and sweaty flight suit all part of his uniform, Major H., a Cobra squadron leader, conducts an impromptu field briefing for his pilots.* Asaf Shilah, BITON HEYL HAVIR was established. Problems did exist, however. Many of the pilots first placed in the helicopter squadron felt as if they were inferior to their fighter pilot counterparts, and many "experienced" IAF officers, such as Mr. HEYL HAVIR himself, Maj. Gen. Ezer Weizman, even went so far as to consider the absorption of helicopters—instead of fighter airplanes—as the death of the IAF. Others, like Col. (Reserves) Eliezer "Cheetah" Cohen, an early commander of the Rotor and the Sword Squadron, as well as the innovative philosopher behind the IDF's use of helicopters for "special operations," had a somewhat different outlook.

"There were several of us who realized that the arrival of the helicopter would drastically alter the make-up of the future battlefield," said Colonel Cohen. "Although a pilot was always taught to provide aerial superiority and support to the combat forces battling for their lives on the ground, the ability to transport supplies, evacuate the wounded, and, after viewing it in Algeria, [fire] antitank missiles were equally as important. Perhaps the acceptance of the helicopter as [an] integral element of the IAF occurred in Ramat Gan Stadium, near Tel Aviv, on Independence Day 1958. Following the 'customary' parachuting of paratroopers onto the stadium's soccer field by means of C-47 Dakotas, the cheering crowds were shocked to hear the pounding thuds of rotor blades and the appearance of two camouflaged S-55s who landed in

Always in constant communication with the ground forces it is airborne to support, a Cobra heads toward *a ground unit patrolling frontier territory.* BITON HEYL HAVIR

78

synch on the grassy soccer field. The helicopters flew directly toward the crowd, then hovered, and then slowly slid to earth; seconds later, a dozen or so heavily armed men were deployed for battle. The helicopters lifted off vertically and quickly; much to the crowd's amusement, they returned after the mock battle was performed in order to evacuate their wounded. From then on, the State of Israel realized what we in the squadron had appreciated for quite some time, that the limitations of the helicopters was the imagination and courage of its pilot!"

By the time the 1967 war erupted into the Arab-Israeli conflict's third major conflagration, the IAF deployed the Alouette-2, several of which were donated to the IAF by generous French Jews; the S-55; the S-58; and, most important, the French-built, three-engined Aerospatiale SA.321 Super Frelon transport masterpiece, which was soon known in IAF jargon as the Super-Helicopter. The Super Frelon was capable of ferrying up to thirty fully armed infantry soldiers—almost twice as many as the sturdy and reliable Sikorsky S-58 could carry—and greatly expanded the IAF's potential use of the choppers in special operations.

Although the Super Frelon, along with the S-58, was used to transport troops and evacuate wounded soldiers during the 1967 fighting—landing paratroopers in Sinai, evacuating the wounded from the West Bank, and helping to seize the Golan Heights from Syria—its service in the 1967-70 1,000 Days War of Attrition secured it legendary status in some of the IDF's most striking and sensitive operations; its range of 820 kilometers (500 miles) made Damascus, Amman, and Beirut easily within its reach.

On December 28, 1968, in retaliation for the hijacking of an El Al flight to Algeria, an elite IDF unit was ferried to Beirut International Airport to punish Lebanon for serving as operations center for Palestinian terrorism; punishment came in the destruction of thirteen Middle East Airlines aircraft. Although the raid, known as Operation TSHURA, "Gift," would not be the last Israeli heliborne visit to Beirut, it did inaugurate a new tool to the Israeli military. For the pilot flying a helicopter, the assignment was no longer thought of as consolation for not being good enough to fly jets, but rather as a new, exciting, and calculating exercise in accuracy, sheer exhilaration, and absolute courage. That operation also introduced another whirlybird superhelicopter to the IAF Order of Battle: the American Bell-205.

The IAF's acquisition of the small, agile, 150 mph American Bell-205 allowed similar, though smaller-scale, operations to be carried out on a day-to-day basis. Nowhere was this illustrated better than in the bitter guerrilla war fought between Palestinian infiltrators and IDF infantry forces in the barren wasteland of the Jordan Valley. Before the arrival of the Bell-205, Bedouin trackers helped IDF units track bands of roaming Palestinian soldiers. The Bell-205 allowed the IAF to do much of the tracking work by air, and once the bandits were spotted, small bands of recon infantry would be lifted in by helicopter for contact and the kill. For the Bell-205 pilots, recently returned from a course in the United States where they learned of the 205's vulnerability to ground fire, flying in the

On a routine patrol of an embattled frontier—the crux between Israel, Syria, and Lebanon—a Cobra makes a low-level pass over friendly armor: a parking lot of MERKAVA MBTs. BITON HEYL HAVIR

79

mountainous desert abyss of the Jordan Valley, amid hails of murderous Palestinian and Jordanian fire was a tremendous display of courage. Navigating in a desert of identical-looking mountains demanded total concentration and skill, as did transporting a squad of riflemen into the heat of battle. For pilots once thought of as the IAF's "second best," their performances were first-rate.

If the agility of the helicopter enabled Israel's special operations to indeed become spectacular, the sheer strength of the Sikorsky CH-53 enabled them to become routine. Larger, more sophisticated, and more reliable than the Super Frelon, the CH-53 became the mainstay heavy transport chopper of the IAF. Yet even before the CH-53—known by the affectionate nickname of YASUR, loosely translated as "Biggest Bird"—was fully integrated within the IDF, it carried out a spectacular military operation. On the night of December 27, 1969, at the height of the War of Attrition, a flight of CH-53s lifted a force of paratroopers from a NA'HA'L, "Fighting

Although it is atypical for an IAF pilot to sport a leather flight jacket, a Defender attack chopper skipper heads out to his aircraft. As the saying goes in the IAF, "Attack chopper pilots are a breed apart from everyone else." BITON HEYL HAVIR

Pioneer Youth" paratroop battalion to the Egyptian radar base at Ras Arab on the Red Sea. Instead of destroying the facility, however, the paratroopers attached cargo straps and harnesses around the base's top-secret Soviet P-12 surface-to-air radar and, with the help of the CH-53, ferried the intelligence prize back to Israel. The raid was known as Operation Chicken 53 and would forever endear the CH-53 with the IAF and the Arab world; cartoons that appeared the following day in the Arab press showed CH-53s in IAF markings whisking the pyramids and the Sphinx back to Israel.

The 1973 Yom Kippur War saw the widespread use of helicopters on both sides. The Syrians deployed Soviet Mi-8 Hip transport choppers to ferry the commandos who seized Mount Hermon in the opening moments of the surprise attack and attempted several daring and audacious landings of large commando units deep behind Israeli lines—including landings at the IDF's Golan Heights Headquarters at Nafekh. The Egyptian Air Force also transported large groups of commando units deep behind Israeli lines by Mi-4 Hounds and Mi-8 Hips fitted with rocket pods.

The IAF was not afforded the "luxury" of initiating offensive heliborne strikes and was forced to make extensive use of its armada of helicopters to transport seriously wounded soldiers from the front lines to hospitals in Israel. The fighting was so fierce that front-line units were unable to evacuate their wounded to rear battalion aid stations, and the helicopter pilots had to land in the middle of ferocious fire-fights and missile-congested battlefields in order to save the badly hurt. Enemy fire was so intense that the door gunners were forced to fire their FN MAGs and .30 caliber machine guns until the barrels melted. Later in the war, however, IAF CH-53s landed a force of reconnaissance paratroopers along the main Damascus-Baghdad road—approximately 100 kilometers (60 miles) from the Syrian capital—to intercept a force of Iraqi tanks heading for the Golan Heights. In the Sinai fighting, CH-53s landed reconnaissance paratroopers atop the heavily defended Egyptian intelligence electronic monitoring station on Jebel A'taka. Many of the IAF heliborne transport operations involving reconnaissance forces remained classified in 1991.

Although the helicopter distinguished itself in the 1973 war—rescuing downed pilots, evacuating wounded, pursuing infiltrating bands of Egyptian commandos, and transporting commandos—its military possibilities were only being discovered. If one *military* lesson was bitterly learned by the IDF in the 1973 war, it was the need for a quick and highly mobile weapon to combat the enemy's overwhelming superiority in armor. That need was filled in the late seventies by the arrival of a sleek, thin, and unassuming-looking aircraft that had tremen-

dous speed, maneuverability, and hellish firepower. That aircraft was the American AH-1 Cobra, a Vietnam-vintage chopper.

The Cobra with its TOW missiles, rockets, and multibarreled guns was soon joined by the Hughes M-D 500 Defender attack chopper—a particularly compact and agile craft—which, with its TOW missiles, chain guns, rocket pods, and even air-to-air missiles, could hold its own against much larger ships and almost any ground target.

Finally, and to the great pride and satisfaction of the offense-geared minds in IAF Headquarters, the agility and capabilities of the helicopter were being used to their max-

With one map in his pocket and another in his hands, the squadron commander, Major C., prepares to *board his five-rotor Defender for a fast and stealthy journey toward the day's target.* BITON HEYL HAVIR

imum potential. Unfortunately, the Syrians too were learning the much-valued and deadly secrets of the attack chopper. The attack chopper, the antitank missile, and Syrian and Israeli forces would all come to a head in Lebanon's true valley of death: the Beka'a Valley.

When the IDF invaded Lebanon on June 6, 1982, according to foreign sources, the IAF's electronic warfare craft, advanced fighter-bombers, and helicopters proved to be a triumvirate of destruction and victory. Once the electronic environment surrounding the Syrian SAM batteries in Lebanon was neutralized to IAF specifications and the F-15s, F-16s, Phantoms, and KFIRS rendered the SAMs and later the MiGs and Sukhois inoperable, Syrian forces on the ground were left with no air cover. With the Levantine skies empty of unfriendlies, the Defender and Cobra choppers were able to snipe away at will at a host of tempting ground targets.

According to Captain N., a Cobra pilot in the 1982 fighting, "Our task was relatively simple. We would hug the earth, fly in tight formation, and attack Syrian armor whenever and wherever we found them. The range of the TOW missile allowed us to fire at them before they could hit us; the TOW was well beyond the limitation of their turret-mounted 14.5 millimeter heavy machine guns. Once their T-62s, T-55s, armored personnel carriers, and supply vehicles were placed in the center of our sights, we put 'just enough' pressure on our missile-release triggers and let the TOW go to work. The rest was technologically inspired, wire-guided destruction."

From their 100 foot altitude perch, the Cobra and Defender pilots watched dozens of camouflaged, Soviet-produced main battle tanks, the pride and glory of the Syrian Army, erupt into disintegrating explosions of shattered armor and engulfing flames. The destruction, in most cases, was systematic and complete.

After having lifted off in formation, a flight of Defenders searches the valleys of southern Israel for the enemy. BITON HEYL HAVIR

The attack helicopters were versatile craft. Not only could they kill enemy tanks, but their ability to take off and land on a dime allowed IDF ground commanders to coordinate attack and defensive strategies with their TOW-wielding guardian angels flying above at a moment's notice. For example, whenever an armored battalion commander wished to confirm an attack plan, the helicopter squadron commander would just park his chopper in the middle of the MERKAVA main battle tank (MBT) and M113 armored personnel carrier (APC) formation, pull out a map, and discuss the impending battle. For an army long known for its armored might, the Cobras and Defenders were proving themselves to be the tanks of the air. The Syrians, however, had their own aerial MBTs.

Just as the Cobras and Defenders were able to unleash deadly accurate TOW missile fire at Syrian tank formations, so too did the Syrian Air Force's armada of Aerospatiale SA.342 Gazelles—armed with the menacing HOT antitank missile—and the Soviet-built Mi-24 Hind, considered by many to be the world's mightiest helicopter gunship. The Syrians first introduced their helicopter gunships in the battle for Ein Zehalta, a mountainous town on the strategic Beirut-Damascus Highway. The Gazelles were able to unleash their HOT missiles from the safe range of 4 kilometers (2.5 miles), often at tree-top level, and inflicted intense panic among the bottlenecked columns of Israeli armor; Israeli tank crews were not equipped with portable antiaircraft missiles, like the Redeye and SAM-7, and the commander's turret-mounted guns were hopelessly outranged. While the Syrian Gazelles inflicted great damage on the IDF's tanks, the devilish beating of the Mi-24's rotor blades and wide array of firepower inflicted panic and impending doom. Indeed, in a region of conflict known for continuous destruction, a new and foreboding age had dawned.

Although the Syrian Air Force was unable to score a single air kill in the war in Lebanon, ground fire did claim several IAF ships—especially choppers. In late June 1982, a Syrian tank shell struck a Defender flying an antitank sortie. It was, in many ways, inevitable retribu-

tion, for during the 1973 war, an Israeli 105 millimeter tank shell downed a Syrian Mi-8 with a similar lucky shot. The Defender had just destroyed several T-62s but suddenly found itself with over thirty shrapnel holes in its engine and helplessly on the ground. The Defender's pilot, Lieutenant Colonel H., saw his second in command, Major G., writhing in pain and bleeding; he prayed for help. Both pilot and navigator were eventually rescued in a daring heliborne operation by a Bell-206 and returned to active service where they flew sorties in the skies over Lebanon.

The advent of the Cobra and Defender revolutionized the IAF's strategic use of air power. Retaliatory air raids against terrorist targets were no longer the sole domain of fighter-bombers. The destruction of a terrorist target could now be entrusted to a flight of Cobras. And the attack helicopter became the mainstay of the IDF's continuous war against Palestinian and Lebanese Shiite terrorists in southern

A Sikorsky CH-53, commonly and affectionately known as the YASUR in IAF jargon, prepares to land off the coast of Damur, Lebanon, during the height of the 1982 Operation Peace for Galilee in Lebanon. Proving invaluable as a heavy transport and air rescue ship, the YASUR pictured here is lifting off, ferrying wounded soldiers back to hospitals in northern Israel. BITON HEYL HAVIR

Lebanon. The Lebanese Mediterranean shores were routinely visited by Defender and Cobra squadrons that searched for terrorist movements, as were Israel's Mediterranean waters; the populated beaches of Tel Aviv, Haifa, and Nahariya were continuously patrolled by the low-flying attack choppers—ensuring that seaborne terrorists who succeeded in slipping through the IDF Navy's shield never reached dry land.

The IAF has taken on new duties with the acquisition of the Aerospatiale AS.365 Dauphin in 1988; the antishipping, maritime patrol, air-sea rescue chopper stationed on IDF Navy missile boats, affectionately called the IAF's Dolphin. The Dolphin became the first and only naval air element of the IDF Navy, but its pilots, aircraft, and tradition were purely IAF.

If the history of helicopters in IAF service has been a success, it has been so up north, along the Purple Line, which separates Israel from Lebanon, where the blue and white rotor blades have had the greatest impact. The attack helicopter, in fact, has become as much a part of the joint-security arrangement that protects the north of Israel from the madness of Lebanon as barbed wire fortifications and the infantryman walking a patrol.

Cobra squadrons based in northern Israel are as much a part of the regular IAF as Phantom or F-15 squadrons, but they are very different. Their base does not consist of elongated runways meant for supersonic aircraft,

IAF crewmen load missiles aboard a newly acquired AH-64 Apache. BITON HEYL HAVIR

comfortable homes, and loving families only a few minutes' drive from their briefing room. Most important, their area of operations leaves the squadron's pilots no room for error. Being a Cobra pilot is 100 percent combat duty. The big show is only a few kilometers away, and takeoff means active duty, as the most routine and basic of patrols could lead to a day filled with combat and death.

For the pilots, the day begins as days begin in every IAF air base: with the squadron commander's briefing. Yet instead of a neat sterile room adorned with glossy photographs, theirs is a small alcove marked by a hand-painted sign in English that says, "The right man for the job!" It is winter, and the harsh Levantine winds make life and flying uncomfortable; the small electronic heater in the room and the heating system inside the cockpit of the Cobra will be the only respites from the cold the pilots will feel today.

Unlike leaders in the "safe" bases in central Israel, Lieutenant Colonel B., the squadron commander, a tall and imposing figure in his sage-green flight suit, addresses his men with a 5.56 millimeter GLILON assault rifle slung over his shoulder. In the briefing, last night's development in southern Lebanon is discussed, as is the new day's latest intelligence offering by the squadron's intelligence officer, who also carries a weapon everywhere he ventures. After the short and concise briefing, the pilots receive their orders and proceed toward their craft. They have little time to waste.

The base in northern Israel is Spartan in comparison with most IAF bases. Armored personnel carriers are strewn about everywhere, as are sandbagged antiaircraft gun positions. Sol-

The seaborne crew of an Aerospatiale AS.365 Dauphin prepares the red-and-white whirlybird for *a mission over the crystal-blue waters of the Mediterranean.* Ofer Karni, IDF spokesman

diers in full combat kit mill about the landing pads, and even the ground crews carry weapons. As the pilots make their way toward their Cobras, the technicians, mechanics, and ground crews are busy ensuring that the ships are in top mechanical form. According to Corporal Moshe, a Cobra mechanic, "You have to take care of this bird with love, compassion, and great care—like a girlfriend." The Cobra ground crews liken the success of their squadron to their efforts on the ground and never allow a ship to take off unless every system has been checked, the weapons are fully loaded, and the fuel tanks are full.

The Cobras are housed in grayish asbestos sheds, where they appear peaceful. The helicopters are painted in a dreary muddy brown—no elaborate eye-catching camouflage schemes, no large IAF Star of David emblems, no colorful squadron insignia. The only large marking is a yellow aerial identification *V* on the fuselage, which lets nervous Israeli soldiers and untrained South Lebanese Army troopers know that the gunship hovering above is *friendly*.

The pilots greet their crews, examine the CAR-15 assault rifles placed in the cockpits, and gear up for a morning's operations; special helmets are fitted, survival vests are donned, and maps are rechecked for one final time. All panels are checked—the scopesight, the throttle stick, the missile and cannon trigger, the fire-control system, the gyroscope, the navigation controls, and, of course, the weaponry. The ship carries four TOW missiles and 7,000 rounds of 7.62 millimeter ammunition for the forward, three-barreled minigun.

For Major R., the pilot of the patrol's lead Cobra, the most important bit of equipment tossed into the cockpit is a tattered blue winter parka, the same one he received in pilot's course. Sentimental good luck articles are an important element of day-to-day life where danger is faced 24 hours per day, seven days per week.

It's a windy day, with northeast gusts coming in at 40 knots. Many of the pilots dislike flying in such weather, but they have no choice. The Cobras must fly in *all* weather conditions. The terrorists venture forth in such weather in the hope of perhaps catching an IDF patrol off guard and ambushing it, or to attempt a border crossing.

Takeoff involves one brown ship after another lifting off in a synchronized choreography. The pounding of the rotor blades engulfs the field; the noise tends to vibrate all ground equipment in a funny way.

Liftoff. Major R.'s Cobra lowers its nose and begins today's flight, which will take it over Galilee, *Fatahland*, and parts of the ever-bustling Golan Heights. The Cobra shakes and pitches in the heavy winds, but Major R. and his forward-sitting number 2, Lieutenant H., manage to glide the sleek aircraft to a smooth flight. Flying at a low level, the Cobra passes countless IDF positions along the heavily fortified northern border: communications posts, infantry positions, and a parking lot neatly crammed with a few dozen MERKAVA MBTs. The sighting of the Cobra sparks the odd wave here and there and constant communications and coordination from the ground expressed in an incessant clattering over the radio.

A few minutes after takeoff, the Cobra hovers over a winding sand road owned by a sole command car and a labyrinth of barbed wire fences. Welcome to the Purple Line.

The one definite about flying over Little Vietnam is the need to be alert. Every tree, rock, and house can hide a terrorist wielding an RPG-7, a SAM-7, or a light machine gun. You don't need much to bring down a chopper—even a heavily armed Cobra—and the terrorists and Israeli pilots realize this. Southern Lebanon appears tranquil from the sky—even from only 40 feet above. The plush green land is tended to meticulously by the farmers, the rolling hills are reminiscent of the Sharon Valley in Israel, and the villages appear day-to-day and harmless. Yet this is Lebanon, and beside those peaceful hills, fertile plains, and harmless homes are thousands of men who are well trained in the art of guerrilla warfare—each home sporting an AK-47, at least. The reality of Lebanon is also never far away. Next to a shiny black Mercedes riding along a winding thoroughfare is a 10 foot deep crater, caused a few years back by a suicide-car bomber. The pilot's eyes peer out of the cockpit with greater intensity.

Flying at a speed of 100 knots at an altitude of 90 feet, the Cobra scans the countryside for signs of trouble. Although their principal missions are reconnaissance and ground support, one of their most successful assignments is deterring Hostile Terrorist Activity (HTA). It is the IAF's version of gunboat—or in this case, gunship—diplomacy.

To the Shiite and Palestinian villages inside the ever active security zone, the low-flying Cobras are a stark reminder as to the presence of the IAF. For the beleaguered Christian villages and South Lebanon Army (SLA) positions, it is a reinforcing boost of morale; SLA positions are frequently attacked in suicidal waves by Shiite guerrillas. The most reassuring sight for the Cobra crew is its own positions on the ground.

A few miles inside the security zone, the Cobra hovers above a small muddy hill held by a force of MERKAVAS and M113 APCs. It is a forward base, and as front-line as one can get without being behind enemy lines. Lieutenant A. waves at the assembled force of armored steel and

Adding extra range and dimension to Israel's overburdened coastal patrol defenses, especially maritime antiterrorist prevention, two Dauphins fly in *formation over the beguiling waters of the Mediterranean.* BITON HEYL HAVIR

then looks at it through the cross hairs of his sights—imagining for just a second what it must be like to face such a force of Syrian armor. For the time being, however, the Cobra crew's main concern remains terrorists. The Cobra dives in, flying only 30 feet above the barren land. Trees, bushes, and people become very clear, as will, hopefully, a terrorist about to fire a weapon.

The patrol takes the Cobra over the volatile Mount Dov area and then east, toward the Golan Heights. The "big one," in Israeli terms, is a war against Syria for the volcanic Golan Plateau, and here is where the next full-scale Arab-Israeli war will probably erupt—where the true capabilities of the Cobra and the courage of its pilots will ultimately be tested.

Flying atop the Golan Heights is mesmerizing for any attack chopper pilot. In 1973, hundreds of Syrian tanks poured across the frontier, attempting to overrun the heights and seize part of northern Israel. In those "primitive" days, the Syrian tanks had to be stopped by the sheer bravery of the Centurion MBT crews serving the legendary 188th and 7th armored brigades and their accurate 105 millimeter guns. The battles, such as the close-quarter struggle of the Valley of Tears, became epic in Israel's history. Every attack helicopter pilot has thought of the opportunity to stem a tide of enemy armored divisions in war. Compared with what the "big one" will be like, the Cobra's and Defender's performances in Lebanon in 1982 were nothing but a side show.

Near the snow-capped peaks of Mount Hermon, the Cobra flies amid dozens of communications and intelligence antennas for the quick hop back to Mount Dov and the Purple Line. The crew has been in the air for almost 2 hours, but work is still to be done. The aircraft cuts across the Purple Line once again and 5 kilometers deeper into Lebanon. Road traffic below brings the Cobra in for a look, but it's all routine and day-to-day for the Lebanese. They are apathetic to their tragic surroundings and accept the pounding of the Cobra's rotor blades as part of their scarred landscape; even the barrel of the Cobra's minigun, which follows the

movements of the pilot's helmet sights, doesn't affect them in the slightest.

After the patrol to the neighboring country up north, the Cobra returns to its base and a mandatory debriefing. In the words of Major T., the Cobra squadron's deputy commander, "Our operational activities in the northern sector can truly be considered special operations. One day's service is never like the next, or the day before. The pilot always knows what takeoffs will be like but, for the life of him, can never predict how it's going to end up: how long the ship will be airborne, if the flight will be chased by enemy fire, if it will be forced to land in enemy territory, or if he'll live to see the next day.

"The nature of the operations [is] almost identical to [that of] those conducted during actual wartime. In this way, the pilots, especially the young ones fresh to the squadron, can acquire important operational experience before being tested in a *big war*. The situations and pressure they encounter can never be duplicated in maneuvers—no matter what the scale—and they force the pilot to choose on the spot among the many options available to him in a combat environment; pressurized decisions in the IAF, especially after pilot's course, are usually correct!

"Also, the nature of flying in northern frontier operations is much different than anything else a helicopter pilot in the IAF will ever encounter. The flight is much looser, free lance when it comes to 'by the book' techniques, and all-weather—the pilot must fly at night, in the rain and in limited visibility. The most important aspect, however, is the pilot's ability to fly in the face of danger. It is a most important attribute the young flyer only receives in operational flights. We usually *absorb* hostile fire of one sort or another, and for the pilot to continue to fly in [the] face of hails of twenty-millimeter tracers is important not only in a psychological level, but in an operational one as well."

The ability of an IAF helicopter pilot to fly in the face of *extreme* danger was illustrated on December 9, 1988, during an audacious and difficult IDF antiterrorist operation. The target was the main headquarters and terrorist training facilities for Ahmed Jibril's notorious Popular Front for the Liberation of Palestine General Command (PFLP-GC) at Na'ameh, just off the Mediterranean coast of Damour, in Lebanon. The raid came a year following the Night of the Hang Glider, an airborne terrorist intrusion into northern Israel that resulted in the death of six infantrymen. In many ways, it also sparked the eventual eruption of the Palestinian uprising in the West Bank and Gaza Strip.

The 1988 IDF attack force consisted of commandos from SAYERET GOLANI, the GOLANI Infantry Brigade's elite reconnaissance force, and landed on the beach by Na'ameh under cover of darkness and marched inland toward its target. The subsequent battle was fierce,

close-quarter, and brutal, with the GOLANI force engaging Jibril's legions in hand-to-hand combat deep inside Vietnamese-designed tunnels. The fighting lasted several hours, and although the GOLANI commandos killed over twenty of Jibril's gunmen, the GOLANI battalion commander, Lt. Col. Amir Meital, was killed. With casualties mounting and daylight presenting a precarious situation, CH-53 YASURS were called in for a quick and, hopefully, uneventful evacuation. The YASURS faced heavy enemy fire, the pilots managing to maneuver the large ships away from the hundreds of flaming projectiles that headed their way. Unfortunately, however, four of the GOLANI fighters, busily engaged by overwhelming enemy forces, were forgotten in the heliborne

Although far from its nautical domain, a Dauphin maritime patrol craft cruises atop the Dome of the *Rock mosque and the Old City of Jerusalem.* BITON HEYL HAVIR

rescue and were left behind. For them, death would have been preferred over being taken prisoner.

The IDF has an unwritten law that soldiers are never left behind, and Chief of Staff Dan Shomron adhered to that mandate; the IAF was summoned. As the YASURS carrying the relieved GOLANI commandos made their way back to Israel, two Cobra gunships flew at full speed for Na'ameh. After providing some hellish cover fire of their own, the Cobras landed in the middle of a frantic battle. They fired incessant bursts of cannon and rocket fire at the encroaching PFLP-GC gunmen, stalling for just enough time to allow each GOLANI fighter to climb aboard one of their four landing skids. Liftoff was made difficult by the additional weight; the commandos clung to their heavy web gear and equipment to avoid a thrashing at the hands of their base quartermaster. Nevertheless, the Cobras took off, and a few hours later, the commandos were back with their unit.

On Air Force Day 1989, Chief of Staff Shomron and IAF commanding officer Ben-Nun awarded four medals of praise to Major N., Major A., Lieutenant M., and Lieutenant D.—the brave young Cobra crews who rescued their GOLANI comrades. In the words of Lieutenant M., "It was as if we were stuntmen in the movie *Blue Thunder* ... appearing out of the blue and saving the day!"

Little could Lieutenant M. have realized how correct his analogy was. For the IAF's helicopter squadrons, the future holds nothing but high-tech mastery, hard work, and continued combat operations. Helicopters such as the Blackhawk are being tested and considered for blue and white service; the *Dauphins*, which are capable of 160 knots, patrol the Mediterranean; and Cobra and YASUR pilots are to be equipped with indigenously designed night vision goggles and HUD helmets. The aged YASUR transport helicopter of Soviet radar and Pyramid fame is being electronically overhauled for service in the twenty-first century; if the Phantom 2000 and the Skyhawk 2000 exist, why not the YASUR 2000? In typical IAF fashion, the best of the past is brought up to the standards of the future, and, in the case of one Cobra that crashed into the Sea of Galilee, damaged craft are rebuilt, redesigned, and made better than ever.

The newest IAF attack helicopter is the McDonnell Douglas AH-64H Apache. On September 12, 1990, in a subdued ceremony at an undisclosed air base in southern Israel, the first batch of Apaches were formally inaugurated into the IAF Order of Battle. Usually the arrival of a new weapon system is met with great anticipation and ceremony. Four months before full-scale war was about to erupt in the Gulf, however, Israel was in no mood for a party. When Prime Minister Yitzhak Shamir, Defense Minister Moshe Arens and IAF commander Maj. Gen. Ben-Nun accepted the first batch of Apaches, they knew they might very well receive their first Israeli baptism of fire in the months ahead, attacking Iraqi targets in a full-scale war.

Chapter 6

The Guardians from Above:
The Aeromedical Evacuation Unit

On this January morning, the tranquil blue Mediterranean wasn't being true to its namesake. Instead of forming placid waves, the waters off the northern Israeli coast were choppy, stormy, and definitely not inviting; to the crew of the IDF Navy DABUR, "Bee," patrol craft anchored in the tumultuous sea, it was clinically known as YAM SHEISH—"Sea Type 6." As the DABUR's commander, a nervous first lieutenant, stood on the sea-swept deck and looked at his diver's watch, the pounding beat of a synchronized visitor was heard in the distance overhead. Moments later, a mammoth CH-53 YASUR, dreary in its mud-brown camouflage scheme, hovered above the small craft; its giant rotors created a powerful and disturbing whirlpool around the small boat.

Just as had been coordinated at headquarters, a "lucky" volunteer from the DABUR, wearing a wet suit and life vest, jumped into the choppy sea to, hopefully, be rescued. His plunge was the signal to the YASUR that two men, looking like spacemen from a B-movie in their bright orange wet suits and shiny white helmets, should be slowly lowered into the stormy waters. After checking the "wounded" sailor's medical condition in a well-rehearsed-though-fastidious manner, the visitors from above fastened the unfortunate volunteer into a stretcher attached to a specially designed winch, invented by the AEU, that was capable of lifting up to 7,700 lb and raised their gloved thumbs to the chopper pilot straight overhead—the signal that ordered the chopper crew, and whatever they happened to be carrying, up. Just as quickly as it had appeared, the YASUR departed for home.

Inside the helicopter, the sailor was "treated and stabilized" by a crew of medics, supervised by a flight surgeon. Though just executing a training endeavor, the helicopter crew attended to their duties with dire seriousness. The completion of this difficult exercise occurred when the YASUR touched down on the landing pad of Haifa's RAM'BAM Hospital and the team commander, Major E., clicked his stopwatch—the smile on his face indicating a job well done.

AEU commandos demonstrate the art of rappelling. In peacetime, it is an easy task; in combat and under enemy fire, it is a fast and hurried process of sheer guts, horror, and, in executing a rescue, dire necessity. Michael Zarfati, BAMACHANE

The joint IDF Navy and IAF exercise was difficult and demanding for the IAF's AEU, which is the most professional, highly trained, integrated, and specialized unit in the IDF's impressive "commando" Order of Battle. It is a secret, elite force of warriors and saviors, specially tasked with the rescue of downed pilots, wounded soldiers, and anyone else in need. Many thankful IAF pilots, who owe their lives to the pilots, mechanics, commandos, medics, and doctors of the AEU, have labeled them "the best of them all."

Almost every air force on earth deploys an elite, medically trained air rescue unit specifically tasked with the rescue of downed pilots. Combat pilots are extremely well trained, dangerously intimate with top-secret hardware and procedures, and often despatched to wage a lone war against enemy targets far from the safety of friendly lines.

For the HEYL HAVIR in its early years, however, long-range operations far from home were nothing more than imaginative visions of the

An AEU surgeon and airborne medic tend to a severely wounded soldier, using the AMSLU, a device that saved countless lives in Lebanon. IDF spokesman

future—and, as a result, no specially trained airborne rescue force existed. The tragically outnumbered IAF could barely hold its own against the combined might of four Arab air forces; its skill and dedication were meant to defend Israeli skies rather than attack faraway Arab targets.

Acquisition of the Mirage, Vatour, and Super-Mystere, as well as the 1967 war, changed everything. Targets as far away as Iraq and Alexandria, in Egypt, were now well within the IAF's grasp, and the likelihood of a plane's, and pilot's, being downed in enemy territory became a reality. The IAF performed brilliantly in that war, however, and, in many cases, pilots shot down over enemy territory soon found themselves greeting the advanced vanguards of IDF armored divisions.

The true marker that indicated the need to form an IAF air rescue force was the brutal War of Attrition—a turning point that transformed the IAF from a "very good" Third World air force to one capable of competing with the "superpower big boys." First, on October 21, 1967, came the opening salvo of the War of Attrition when the flagship of the IDF Navy, the destroyer INS EILAT, was attacked by an Egyptian aircraft, which fired Soviet-built Styx sea-to-sea missiles, and sunk off the coast of Sinai. Many of the EILAT's 199 sailors were killed in the explosions and fires caused by the missile volley; others were badly burned and in dire need of emergency medical care.

The IAF duly despatched several Super Frelon helicopters to pick up the dead and wounded, often making gallant attempts to pluck them out of flaming waters amid the chaos of enemy fire and cries of anguish, but the Super Frelon crews were combat flyers, *not* rescuers or medics. As a result, the badly hurt had to be transported to a makeshift aid station on the Sinai shoreline for emergency care before being sent to a hospital back in Israel. Although 152 of the EILAT crew members were saved by the Super Frelon pilots, many have argued that the delay in bringing immediate medical attention contributed to the final death toll of forty-seven sailors.

The sinking of the EILAT had numerous military, as well as political, repercussions. In IAF Headquarters the effective heliborne rescue began to play in the minds of some innovative operational planners who appreciated the need for a specially trained force of heliborne warriors and healers to be on call for such tragic eventualities.

But the sinking of the flagship was just one military reality of the full-scale bloodletting of the War of Attrition. Another reality was long-range aerial bombings of targets deep inside Egypt. When Soviet-produced and, toward the end of the three-year conflict, Soviet-manned surface-to-air missile batteries and radar-guided guns began to blast the IAF aerial bombers out of the sky, still another reality was the capture, killing, and wounding of pilots far beyond Israel's borders.

Although the creation of a specially trained air rescue force was an impossible task during wartime, dozens of pilots were eventually rescued by helicopter. One spectacular rescue occurred on June 30, 1970, when two F-4E Phantoms attacking an Egyptian SAM battery were shot down. In all, four chutes opened; the pilot and navigator from the first ship were captured, as was the pilot from the second ship. Only the navigator from the number 2 Phantom managed to manipulate his chute *away* from the pursuing Egyptian forces and hails of AA fire—the Egyptians even fired a SAM-2 at him!—to reach tentative safety. His only hope for rescue was a small, though powerful, communications and homing device that faithfully transmitted a code back to his home base.

At night, when chances of a helicopter's succumbing to ground fire were minimal, a chopper was despatched to bring the navigator, or his body, back to Israel. Flying blind, straight into the Egyptian Army's front-line position, was an act of great courage for the chopper's crew, but reaching the enemy's front line was the easiest third of the night's mission; they still had to find the pilot—his device had a range finder margin for error of 200 meters—retrieve him, and put it into gear for the "bumpy" hop back to Sinai.

Captain T., the chopper's pilot, described the mission: "[It was like] finding an electronic needle in a haystack laying atop a time bomb, but some lucky flying and the navigator's courage allowed us to find him without *too* much difficulty. It was too dark for us to see him, however, and we couldn't have known that he

An AEU chopper assists another elite unit, the IDF Navy's HA'KOMMANDO HA'YAMI, "naval commandos," during breathtaking training maneuvers in the Mediterranean. According to Colonel Z., a senior officer at IDF Navy Headquarters, "Our cooperation and mutual reliance are both essential and highly successful." BITON HEYL HAVIR

93

had buried his flashlight with his gear after bailing out."

When the signal from the communications device came in as clear as it could transmit, but still nothing was spotted, Captain T. realized that he would never find the navigator in the pitch-black desert. Courageously, he decided to do what he had been strictly ordered *not to* back at base: illuminate the ship's two projector lamps onto the desert hills below. The lights helped locate the appreciative navigator and, at first, surprised the Egyptians. Incessant AA fire soon followed, however, and only Captain T.'s zigzag evasive flight pattern allowed the chopper to escape the splintering glow of 30 millimeter tracer fire and make it back home. In Israel, Captain T. witnessed the reunion of the navigator with his expecting wife and thanked the Almighty for the reliability of his helicopter.

The advent of the transport chopper—the Super Frelon, the CH–53, and the Bell-205—into the IAF arsenal should have meant the formation of a special air rescue unit during the War of Attrition, but it didn't. A training accident involving the destruction of two Phantoms, and

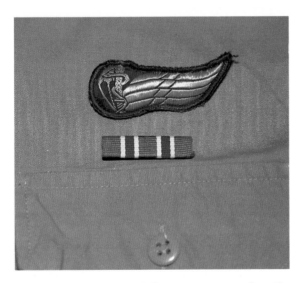

The AEU wings and the Lebanon war campaign ribbon, worn proudly on the chest of one of the unit's own. Sigalit Katz

the IAF's subsequent and unprofessional rescue attempt in the Gulf of Aqaba, near the Red Sea resort town of Eilat, did, however. The incident gave birth to the AEU. The outbreak of the 1973 Yom Kippur War delayed the formation of such a unit by one year, even though countless dramatic helicopter rescues of downed pilots stranded behind enemy lines were executed during the conflict. Oddly enough, when the IAF created the AEU—or, as it's known to the natives, YECHIDAT HACHILUTZ SHEL HEYL HAVIR—in 1974, the IAF commander was Maj. Gen. Benjamin "Benny" Peled, a flyer who, in the 1956 Sinai Campaign, was himself shot down by ground fire behind enemy lines and rescued by a Piper Cub.

When the HEYL HAVIR produced its AEU, IAF Headquarters was determined to produce something much more than a clone of one of the many reconnaissance commando units in the IDF's green, or army, inventory. It had to be a *special forces* unit in the truest definition of the word: combat proficient, cohesive, and able to reach and exit any enemy objective; a heliborne trauma center of well-trained doctors and medics able to administer the most sophisticated medical attention; and all-weather and on call 24 hours per day, because pilots are shot down, soldiers are wounded in a fire-fight, and civilian accidents occur without prior notification.

To form such a unit, the AEU had to produce its own indigenous supermen. First, it had to recruit and attract volunteers, mainly among bored veteran officers and NCOs from other IDF SAYEROT, "reconnaissance formations," as well as new conscripts: idealistic eighteen year olds, who would be willing and able to undergo over a year of hell and sign on an additional few years of military service as professional soldiers in a demanding unit. The AEU also needed a special breed of medical personnel to volunteer—flight surgeons and doctors in search of a challenging change to their careers. According to Lieutenant Colonel B., a thirty-nine-year-old flight surgeon and helicopter pilot, as well as one-time AEU commander, the response to "the call for volunteers, initially, was so great that our ranks were filled quite quickly—I was even forced to tell friends who graduated with me in medical school and ahead of me in officer's course that we didn't need any more personnel."

Training in the AEU lasts over a year and is probably the most arduous, demanding, and all-inclusive in the IDF. The AEU team members have to be a little bit of everything. They have to be expert medics to support the team's flight surgeon; first aid and cardiopulmonary resuscitation (CPR) are much-honed staples of AEU training. As many of their rescue attempts must be made in enemy territory, amid a flurry of projectile and warhead activity, the AEU team members have to be expert soldiers, able to make it toward a wounded pilot's or soldier's position as well as to hightail it out of there in haste; they are trained to be intimate, comfortable, and deadly with every type of weapon—Israeli, Soviet, American, European, and "other"—found within the IAF's range, a geographical limit that, although classified, includes many countries throughout the Middle East and parts of Europe, Asia, and Africa.

All AEU soldiers must know how to kill as well as heal. Because the Israeli military operations are carried out almost daily and pass well beyond the boundaries of the State of Israel, the AEU must perform under all climatic and geographic conditions. Its personnel are full-fledged static-line and HALO paratroopers; expert rappellers and mountaineers; well-trained drivers, skiers, cold-weather survivalists, scuba divers, and sailors; and superb swimmers. They are also expert at demolitions; when a pilot—and plane—are downed, AEU commandos must know just how much explosive it will take to obliterate a top-secret aircraft before the enemy comes to retrieve it. They also have to know the intricacies of antipersonnel and antitank land mines. Most important, perhaps, the AEU's pilots and ground crews must be the best the IAF can field—able to fly and maintain helicopters for long-range operations, in conditions ranging from the brutal heat of the Negev Desert to the snowy cold of the Lebanon mountain range.

The AEU's primary mode of transportation is the helicopter—the Bell-212 and the CH-53

YASUR—although it deploys from fixed-wing aircraft, such as the C-47 Dakota and C-130 Hercules. Its aircraft are airborne operating rooms and miniarsenals, equipped with a wide variety of both medical and offensive military hardware, which enables them to be ready to handle any eventuality at a moment's notice.

The type of aircraft deployed depends on the type of incident the AEU is called to, as well as on the condition of the patient. The flight surgeons, for example, prefer the Super Frelon for delicate injuries because it is big and comfortable, quiet with a steady flight, and relatively free from oil leaks. The Bell-212 and YASUR are more maneuverable, but they tend to vibrate too much in flight—making the performance of some delicate medical procedures a precarious undertaking. Everyone, however, eagerly awaits the arrival of the Sikorsky UH-60A Blackhawk—which will be the AEU's airborne Rolls-Royce—should it eventually be acquired.

The Bell-212 is the AEU's primary workhorse, especially since it is equipped with the Air

As the AEU's domain includes every climatic, military, and geographic scenario, great emphasis is placed on pilot-rescue training in all situations. Here, AEU commandos signal the end to a successful sea rescue with a red smoke grenade and flaming flare. BITON HEYL HAVIR

With the DABUR's crew looking on in awe around the starboard's 20 millimeter Oerlikon cannon, a ship's crewman is brought onboard an AEU's hovering YASUR during the AEU's version of "live-fire" rescue training. BITON HEYL HAVIR

Mobile Life Support Unit (AMLSU), a system specifically designed by the IDF's HEYL REFUAH, "Medical Corps." The AMLSU transforms a helicopter into a flying coronary intensive care unit. It contains oxygen storage of approximately 520 gallons and respiratory resuscitation equipment; a cardiac monitor and defibrilator; suction and aspiration equipment; and auxiliary equipment for illumination, storage, and control. Besides being advanced, it is a practical device. It can perform cardiac monitoring and defibrilation on one patient, positive pressure ventilation of two patients, and oxygen enrichment to two others—simultaneously! The AMLSU has already saved dozens of lives, including those of three seriously wounded soldiers in Lebanon.

The AEU's versatile equipment allows the unit to be mobile and fast: endearing qualities when the difference between life and death can be measured in seconds. In peacetime, the AEU is spread out among several air bases in Israel. When the siren is sounded and the crews race toward the awaiting choppers, they have no idea whether they are going to be rescuing an injured KFIR pilot who has been shot down by SAMs over Lebanon or the victims of a terrorist incident in a northern frontier town. They get a priority takeoff from the control tower *every* time. Only after they are airborne does the pilot get the first tidbits of information regarding where he'll be flying to and what his crew will be doing.

Until 1982, most of the AEU's *combat* expertise went untested. The unit's Bell–212s had hovered amid blinding clouds of smoke, and rescuers dangled by rope into a fiery hell while freeing tourists from an inferno in the luxurious Hotel Moriah on the shores of the Dead Sea; they had saved dehydrated and critically injured hikers who fell down deep crevices in the Negev Desert; and, until Israel's pullout from the Sinai Desert, they had delivered countless bouncing baby girls and boys from Bedouins who trusted no doctor other than "the masked medicine men who arrived by flying monster." All that changed on June 6, 1982. For the AEU, as for much of the IAF in the eighties, the moment of truth came in Lebanon, during Operation Peace for Galilee.

On the first day of the war, a day that was particularly brutal for the IAF, the AEU executed a spectacular rescue. During the late morning blitz, an IAF Skyhawk was downed by a SAM-7; the pilot's body was seized by the Palestinian terrorists who shot him down, savagely mutilated, and then, to the delight of television news crews, paraded through the streets of the city of Sidon—dangling out of a car trunk. In the afternoon, a Bell-212 AEU chopper flying over the Nabatiyeh Plateau, in southern Lebanon, was hit by Palestinian ground fire and shot down; all five crew members were killed.

Later that night, the AEU unit commanded by Lieutenant Colonel R., from the same Bell-212 squadron of the ship downed earlier, was assigned a mission: gravely wounded soldiers from the SAYERET GOLANI task force—the reconnaissance commando battalion of the 1st GOLANI Infantry Brigade—who had participated in the capture of Beaufort Castle a few hours earlier were awaiting the medevac trip back to a hospital in northern Israel. The battle for Beaufort Castle was still going, however; mopping-up operations were still underway and the area was still very hot. To make matters worse, the precise location of the wounded GOLANI commandos was not known. To add to an already tense situation that was developing in Lieutenant Colonel R.'s Bell-212, they'd be flying into the same aerial zone in which the Bell-212 flown by their friends had been blown out of the sky.

Even though such a rescue was something rehearsed in training thousands of times, nothing is like the real thing: the TACHLIS! The skies were cloudy and visibility was minimal. The Bell-212 landed and pulled up at several rendezvous points, only to find no friendly forces anywhere in the immediate vicinity. Radio communications with the GOLANI force failed to establish its exact coordinates, and the rescue pilots were forced to locate it by a slow, nerve-racking, low-altitude search below the safety of cloud cover. After 30 minutes of searching, under intense Palestinian ground fire, the Bell-212 finally spotted the GOLANI fighters. The AEU crew hastily loaded the wounded on board,

attended to their medical conditions, and shot like the devil out of Lebanon.

During the flight back to Israel, and a hospital in Safed, the Bell-212 found itself the target of incessant gun and missile fire. Major F., one of the 212's pilots, found himself maneuvering in and out of tracer lines, under and above mortar shells, and amid a whole host of lights and explosions even his trained eye couldn't identify. To shore up his—as well as the rest of the crew's—courage, he was heard joking over the radio, "I don't think they like us up here." For the following 12 hours, Lieutenant Colonel R.'s Bell-212—and a few other aircraft from the squadron—shuttled back and forth to southern Lebanon to evacuate dozens of other seriously wounded soldiers.

Later that year, Lieutenant Colonel R.'s crew was cited by Maj. Gen. David Ivry, the IAF commanding officer during Operation Peace for Galilee, "for dedication to mission in the face of hazardous ground fire and equally hazardous atmospheric conditions, and for demonstration of high standards of professional skill." Lieuten-

Heading out toward a rendezvous with a DABUR patrol craft, an AEU YASUR lowers its altitude and speed a few miles out in the Mediterranean. BITON HEYL HAVIR

ant Colonel R. viewed this appreciation as a loud and clear message to the soldiers on the ground that should they ever find themselves in a situation where they need help from above, the AEU will spare no effort to evacuate them to a hospital as quickly as humanly possible. In Lieutenant Colonel R.'s words, "If we succeed in alleviating some of the anxiety of our forces on the ground, we have more than performed our mission."

Other AEU teams proved just as impressive in Lebanon. During the first four months of Operation Peace for Galilee, eighty-five percent of Israeli casualties were evacuated by air for the 1 hour flight back to Israel; a total of 2,518 medevac trips were made by chopper—a marked accomplishment compared with the 1973 war when only thirty percent of the Israeli

wounded were medevaced. Sometimes, the severity of a soldier's wounds did not afford AEU pilots the "luxury" of the hour ride back to Israel, and they had to fly to a safe location somewhat removed from the fighting; the flight surgeons performed emergency surgery in the field while shells landed nearby, and AEU personnel took up firing positions to protect the impromptu operating room from enemy attack.

For many AEU doctors, reservists brought into the fray for a month or two annually, the transition was sharp and dramatic. Only days earlier, they were wearing white lab coats, treating common colds, and tending to fussy patients in clinics in Tel Aviv, Jerusalem, or Haifa. Now, in *the unit*, with their flight coveralls, full battle kit, personal weapon, and commando knife, they

July 6, 1989. After an Islamic fundamentalist terrorist pushed a crowded Tel Aviv-Jerusalem intercity commuter bus off a 200 foot high cliff, AEU choppers *transport the most seriously hurt to hospitals in Jerusalem. Fifteen were killed in this terrorist act.*

are performing lifesaving emergency surgical procedures on a slab of dirt in Lebanon, trying to stabilize a body ripped by shrapnel so that a wounded soldier can survive the flight back to Israel.

The difficult psychological transition for the citizen-soldier-reservist relies on a built-in human strength that the AEU's intense preacceptance screening process hopes to, but can't always, determine in a candidate. According to Major D., a senior flight surgeon and seasoned veteran of countless Lebanon sorties, "We try desperately hard to draw the fine golden line between the quickness of the evac and what's medically safe. That golden line also separates the civilian doctors from the reservist [or] career AEU flight surgeon."

AEU rescues were not limited solely to IDF personnel; severely wounded Lebanese citizens, Syrian soldiers, and Palestinian terrorists were also lifted by helicopter out of Lebanon to Israeli hospitals. The end of Operation Peace for Galilee did not end the IDF's involvement in Lebanon, however, and AEU operations continued—as always, around the clock. The AEU's all-encompassing training paid invaluable dividends in the difficult climatic conditions encountered in Israel's neighbor up north—bitter cold and blizzard snows in the winter and brutal heat in the summer—with AEU teams forced to use all their specialized gear.

Perhaps the AEU's most pressing day in Lebanon was on May 4, 1988, when a large IDF paratrooper force attacked the Shiite—*Hizbollah*-held—village of Maidun, in southeastern Lebanon, in retaliation for *Hizbollah*'s assistance to numerous Palestinian attempts to infiltrate suicide terrorist squads into northern Israel. The battle was so fierce that many firefights were conducted at pointblank ranges, the Shiite gunmen not surrendering their positions until they were martyred by superior IDF firepower. Three Israeli paratroopers were killed in the chaos and seventeen were seriously wounded. Each Israeli casualty was medevaced to safety by the AEU, its Bell-212s landing on numerous occasions into murderous hails of Shiite machine gun and cannon fire. Exchange of fire was so incessant that many of the door gunners ran out of 7.62 millimeter ammunition for their FN MAGs. Many senior IAF commanders consider the AEU's performance at Maidun to be the unit's most difficult test, and one of its most shining successes.

On the quiet days, where no news from Lebanon is good news—what's basically known in Israel as peacetime—the AEU is always on alert and always ready. Peacetime does not bring a much-needed vacation to the unit, however. Training exercises, civilian accidents, and other dangerous situations always require its attention. When a hiker realizes he cannot get down from a mountain he has scaled in the Arava Desert, the AEU plucks him to safety. When a severe traffic accident occurs on Israel's chaotic roads, the AEU is the first one called; its ability to pry a victim loose from mangled steel impresses even the most experienced civilian firefighters and paramedics. And when an organ is needed for a transplant, AEU pilots are offered the chance to become high-flying, high-speed, aerial taxi drivers.

Military training accidents and mishaps also need to be contended with. Recently on maneuvers, a commando from a reconnaissance unit fell into a sand pit that was over 25 feet deep. Soldiers from the unit tried in vain to extract their comrade from the hole, but he was seriously hurt from the fall and not responding to their attempts. Finally, the AEU was summoned. To the awe of the commandos on the ground, a flight surgeon was lowered into the deep pit and came out moments later with the wounded soldier safely in a specially designed folding stretcher. At last report, both soldier and unit were doing fine.

During the bloody apex of the *Intifadah*, or Palestinian uprising in the West Bank and Gaza Strip, the AEU was operational and active almost 24 hours per day, evacuating both Palestinian and Israeli wounded to hospitals.

The appetency for the AEU to execute such difficult and delicate missions comes as a result of the high quality of volunteers. Historically, the AEU sought its personnel from new conscripts at the IDF's main recruitment depot, but according to the unit's comander in the early nineties, Major N., "We've gone away from the traditional method of seeking potential volunteers for being a combat rescuer in our unit, by searching computer files, by now seeking those soldiers who find themselves suddenly expelled from pilot's course and still very much wanting to remain in the Air Force. Not to say that all ex-pilot cadets are suitable for AEU service, but we generally find in them a motivational high and a desire to prove themselves [that] few other Israeli soldiers can emulate."

The doctors, on the other hand, are interesting enigmas. They have to be studious geniuses, able to master basic medicine and emergency trauma care, as well as Rambo-like commandos, able to fire dozens of different weapons, march endless kilometers, scale steep cliffs, and then find the wherewithall to administer expert medical care to a critically hurt individual. The doctors, elitist and temperamental persons in any culture, love the thrill and danger. This is especially true with the reservists who check out hernias one afternoon and save a downed and frostbitten pilot the next.

Recently, the AEU has proven that it is an integrated as well as elitist military force with its first female flight surgeon. Capt. Miri Markin—better known in the unit as Dr. Miri—is thirty years old. Having advanced through medical

En route toward a sea rescue training mission, a Bell–212 in AEU service races along Israel's northern Mediterranean coastline. BITON HEYL HAVIR

school, IDF officer's course, and AEU training, she is considered "one of the boys"; proving herself and her determination in the field, she eventually reached the command of an AEU team.

Dr. Miri finds herself airborne more frequently than she had ever thought possible. Stationed at a base housing several fighter and bomber squadrons, her team faces the always-present possibility of being called upon to rescue a downed pilot. Not all pilot rescues involve a daring foray behind enemy lines. When, for example, two or three wheels in the landing gear of an F-16C or D fail to open or lock and a Hydrozine emergency develops, their AEU chopper becomes airborne in minutes.

One incident that had tragic results came from a new type of terrorism. It was terrorism without hostages, explosives, or gunfire, but destructive nevertheless. On July 6, 1989, the crowded-to-capacity bus number 405, the intercity bus whose route connects bustling Tel Aviv with the capital, Jerusalem, was traveling along the narrow twisting mountain highway on its routine run. At a critical juncture along the road, a twenty-two-year-old Gazan belonging to the shadowy Islamic Jihad terrorist group leapt from his seat, began to shout "Allahu Akbar," "God is great," raced toward the driver's compartment, and forced the driver to veer off the leveled roadway down a 200 foot deep gully. The bus crashed and erupted into a fiery hell.

As the wounded attempted to escape the inferno, several IAF helicopters appeared in the dust-clouded sky and landed inside the death-filled ravine. No sooner had the choppers landed than medics and doctors from the AEU raced toward the accident to try to save those who could be saved. They quickly determined who would die and who had a chance to live, placed them aboard their airborne ambulances, and flew at top speeds toward a hospital in Jerusalem. Although the final toll was fifteen dead and twenty-seven wounded, the men of the AEU made a tragic incident less fatal for a good many innocents.

In a letter to Maj. Gen. Avihu Ben-Nun, commanding officer of the IAF, Israeli defense minister Yitzhak Rabin praised the AEU for its "professionalism, courage and dedication in saving the lives of so many." The defense minister's long-overdue commendation was, oddly enough, the first *public* mention of the AEU to many military-savvy Israelis. For the volunteer supermen and superwomen of the AEU, saving lives from the most impossible combat and climatic situation has been a duty they've been faithfully executing for well over fifteen years.

A group of men who will be executing such tasks for the next fifteen years are the graduates

An AEU hopeful prepares her gear for a "routine" training flight in a Bell-212. Michael Zarfati, BAMACHANE

of MAHZOR SHVA-ESRAI, the AEU's seventeenth class of commando rescuers. The graduation ceremony is highly charged and extremely impressive. A few dozen men, wearing their khaki Air Force Class A uniforms, assemble at an air base in central Israel to get their reward for the arduous hardships they've endured, survived, and overcome: the AEU's navy-blue and silver cloth wings. The design of these wings illustrates the unit's triumvirate of responsibilities: a sword for its combat prowess; a parachute for its airborne capabilities; and a snake for its medical tasks.

Major N., the unit's commander, informs his newest subordinates, "Your work and responsibilities as a combatant and savior of lives have only just begun. Never underestimate the importance of your task." N. knows this from personal experience. As a company commander in SAYERET GOLANI following much service in Lebanon, he was critically wounded in a traffic accident involving his jeep and a jackknifed bus. Although almost killed, N. not only rehabilitated, but returned to military service to command one of Israel's most prestigious units. Although still considered handicapped by the IAF, N. leads every rescue his immediate unit is called upon to execute.

As the new rescuers parade on the tarmac for the assembled top brass and proud family members, show time begins; several of the craft that will be their airborne homes for the next few years, Bell–212s and YASURS, perform acrobatic maneuvers that impress everyone. A YASUR performs several sharp turns and then flies almost directly into the crowd, before pulling up

and landing as softly as a feather. Moments later, a red smoke grenade explodes and a Bell–212 appears. As the 212 hovers above the tarmac, four AEU soldiers, two hanging out of each side of the chopper, grasp onto ropes and rappel down onto the ground. Applause erupts from the crowd as the newly inducted commandos realize that this is what they'll now be doing for a living.

What they'll also be doing for a living is teaching pilot candidates—the men they are eventually supposed to protect—how to survive. On a sun-swept beach in southern Israel, a group of pilot candidates from the Advanced Basic stage of the course have assembled for an exhilarating lesson in the art of survival: what to do when one is forced to parachute into the sea. The cadets will be taken to the open ocean by a Navy tug and then sent adrift with only their life vests to keep them afloat. Then, the Bell–212 will appear and introduce them to the art of being plucked out of the sea by the AEU. Before commencing the exercise, First Lieutenant C., the chief AEU medic this afternoon, informs the pilot cadets that "the only thing which a pilot who lands over water *must* do is *not* drown; we'll take care of the rest." That comment invokes a reassuring smile from the cadets as well as their instructor, an experienced pilot in his own right.

That trust between pilot and air rescue commando allows the pilot to concentrate on his HUD panel, his controls, his multimillion-dollar jet, and, most important, his mission. Not having to worry about what will happen if he's shot down is a hidden element behind the IAF's superb performance in Israel's wars.

Chapter 7

Half Blue, Half Green: The Air Defense Forces

And though they climb up to heaven,
thence will I bring them down.
—Amos 9:2; the motto of the Air Defense Forces

The Syrian MiG–27 Flogger-D flew a level path over the hills of central Israel. Its swept wings, camouflaged in a practical sand and olive-drab scheme, were set for attack position; the underwing-mounted fuel tanks indicated that the aircraft had traveled a long way to reach its target. That target, an IAF air base on full alert, was defended by a whole host of anti-aircraft guns and missiles, although today, a Bofors L–70 Super-Fledermause 40 millimeter gun would take a turn defending its immediate skies.

As the MiG began its attack dive, the 40 millimeter gun's fire controller tracked it and the gunner placed the Syrian Air Force's red, white, and black roundels into his sights and awaited the order to fire. Time was running out, but still no authorization was received from the battery commander. Finally, as the gunner's leg tensed on the foot-pedal trigger mechanism, the order of ESH, "fire," was received over the communications piece. The volley of 40 millimeter projectiles was deafening and accurate. After absorbing approximately six direct hits, the MiG–27 was destroyed. The air base had been saved.

The MiG–27's pilot didn't bail out because the MiG–27 had no pilot. It was a motorized toy—a target drone named EDO, in memory of three air defense soldiers killed at the gates of Beirut in 1982—painted in Syrian colors, maneuverable, in scale to the real thing, and meant to provide realistic target practice to the gunners and missile operators of the IAF's Air Defense Forces, known in Hebrew by the acronym NUN-MEM, "Anti-Aircraft." As unheralded an organization as could be found in the Israeli military, the Air Defense Forces have executed their primary task of protecting Israel's vulnerable population centers and strategic targets with skill, courage, and technological innovation. Although they are known in Israel as the IAF's infantry, they are as much a part of the modern IAF as its pilots, their supersonic fighters, and their attack helicopters.

The true roots of the Air Defense Forces date back to May 15, 1948, when a Spitfire Mk. 9 of the Royal Egyptian Air Force was shot down over the Sde Dov airfield north of Tel Aviv by a 20 millimeter Hispano-Suiza gun. What the Israeli gunners, teenage survivors of the Holocaust who had undergone an intensive five-day training course, lacked in conditioning they more than made up for in spirit. A 20 millimeter gun like the Hispano-Suiza was considered heavy artillery by the newly formed IDF, however, and, accordingly, the task of defending the Israeli skies was given to the Artillery Corps. It was a mixed marriage that wouldn't last forever.

Initially, the Air Defense Forces were considered bottom of the barrel. Because they were dispersed among Israel's few IAF bases, permanent and somewhat "quiet" positions, their ranks were filled by soldiers too old or physically unfit for combat duty, as well as those who, for personal reasons, needed to serve close to home. Besides their very real human resources shortcomings, the Air Defense Forces also suffered from a power struggle between the black berets of the Artillery Corps (the owners of the Air Defense units) and the blue berets (the owners of the IAF air bases where the Air Defense Forces were deployed).

In 1962, the American-made Hawk surface-to-air missile was acquired by the Artillery Corps to help defend IAF bases, now increasingly within the range of Soviet-supplied aircraft flown by Arab air forces. At the time, the Hawk was a technologically advanced and awe-inspiring weapons system. Painted in a white and black design, with a large royal-blue IAF Star of David decorating its fins, the missile appeared to be more a symbol of might and speed than a defense against medium- and low-altitude intruders. The Hawk batteries, perched amid the takeoffs and landings of IAF fighters and bombers, convinced many that the role of air defense should belong solely to the HEYL HAVIR, especially considering that the IAF possessed the logistic and technical support apparatus needed to maintain such sophisticated missile and radar systems. Like many things in the ever-changing military picture of the Middle East, the IAF, the

Action time for a Vulcan crew across the Purple Line. With only stars and starlight scopes for illumination, a Vulcan keeps up its end of the joint-security arrangement in a dangerous spot of the world. BITON HEYL HAVIR

Hawk, and the Air Defense Forces would change dramatically in the years to come.

When the IAF launched its blitz against Egyptian, Jordanian, Syrian, and Iraqi air bases to begin the 1967 Six Day War, it appeared as if the Hawk operators and 40 millimeter AA gunners would have no work at all. On the second day of the war, however, an Iraqi Air Force Tupelov Tu–16 bomber penetrated Israeli airspace and bombed the coastal city of Netanya. A few minutes later, a 40 millimeter AA battery stationed in northern Israel, near Megiddo, received word that the large, high-flying intruder would be passing its position.

The battery, commanded by Lt. Yisrael Shar'el of Netanya, was brand-new; it had been in place less than two weeks and was manned by recruits who, because of the mobilization of all Israeli men before the war, had yet to undergo basic training. Nevertheless, in the short time he had them, Lieutenant Shar'el trained his crews well. The Tupelov was tracked by the battery's radar guidance system, locked, and, in a deafening flurry of projectiles, destroyed, its shattered fuselage falling over the Jezreel Valley. In celebration of downing the Iraqi bomber, Lieutenant Shar'el shared a bottle of chilled champagne with over ninety of his men.

The Six Day War expanded the boundaries of the State of Israel significantly; the subsequent War of Attrition spread the Israeli warplanes dangerously thin. The Egyptians, in particular, took advantage of this weakness by staging hit-and-run attacks with small units, as well as low-level strafing runs with MiG and Sukhoi fighter-bombers; the isolated and lightly gunned Israeli positions were helpless against these attacks.

On May 21, 1969, however, one such attack met an unexpected aerial barrier. A Hawk battery's radar managed to lock onto a MiG–21 that had just taken off from an air base near Port Said. The siren at the Hawk position was sounded, the troopers raced toward their positions, and authorization was requested to blow the MiG out of the sky. The OK was received, the launch button was pushed, and, seconds later, the MiG–21 disintegrated—the victim of a direct hit. Within the battery, in Artillery Corps headquarters, and in the IAF nerve center, news of the first kill for an Israeli Hawk was greeted with great celebration. Great happiness also was felt in the United States, and in Raytheon's corporate headquarters because the MiG–21 was the world's first "kill" for the Hawk missile.

Another first in Israeli air defense occurred on February 21, 1970. The Egyptian Air Force, after suffering heavy losses at the hands of IAF Mirage and Phantom pilots, attempted a new and, for a time, effective strategy: strafing Israeli positions in Sinai at sunset, when the sun would be in the defenders' eyes. Israel Aircraft Industries was called upon to invent a mobile, high-powered AA gun to counter this new tactic, and its response was brilliant in its simplicity. Technicians at IAI took a captured Egyptian BTR armored car with an American armored turret and attached to it two 20 millimeter cannons—cannibalized from an obsolete Ouragan jet. It was a novel idea that few officers ever expected to work—expressed in that the crews that were supposed to operate these bastardized guns received less than 24 hours of training on them.

On February 21, two Egyptian MiG–17s appeared out of the setting sun, rocketing and bombing an Israeli position. The twin 20 millimeter guns tracked the intruders and, in accurate bursts of manual fire, downed both of them! The twin-mounted guns, later deployed on dozens of different types of armored vehicles that IAI technicians "liberated" from IDF Ordnance Corps parking lots, endeared itself with the nickname Little Monster and killed dozens more aircraft in the years of conflict that followed.

By December 1970, the Air Defense Forces were finally transferred to HEYL HAVIR control. Initially and contrary to most predictions, the transfer was difficult. The combat and front-line soldiers of the Air Defense Forces—who wore the green (army) uniforms of the Artillery Corps, carried UZIS like any other combat soldier, and wore the black beret with red (combat) background—were incensed by their new predicament: wearing the khaki uniforms and blue berets of JOBNIKS (male soldiers in noncombat assignments), and being trapped in a corps

where, the conception was, being a pilot is everything and the only thing. For the first few years, in fact, Air Defense soldiers about to leave their bases on weekend passes quickly changed back into their old olive fatigues, compromising only by agreeing to wear the IAF beret. They were field soldiers true and through and needed the appreciation that came with that unique and

A future M163 Vulcan gunner learns the ins and outs of the weapons system he'll be operating, managing, and commanding for the next 33 months—its vehicle, 20 millimeter gun (at both 1,000 and 3,000 rounds per minute), and always-to-be-pushed 300 mile range. BITON HEYL HAVIR

well-deserved distinction. That needed appreciation came in the form of the 1973 war, a conflict where every Israeli unit, no matter what uniform its members wore, was put to its most dire test.

During the Yom Kippur War, the Air Defense Forces of the HEYL HAVIR performed brilliantly. Forced to operate *without* the IAF owning the skies, the NUN-MEM units encountered Syrian and Egyptian pilots who were bolder, flew better aircraft, and were not intimidated by 40 millimeter cannons and Hawk missiles.

Under IAF tutelage, however, the AA units were pounded, molded, and refined into a top-rate combat force. Basic training marches were increased from 20 to 75 kilometers (12 to 47 miles), every bit of their cherished uniform had to be paid for with sweat and hard labor, and their weapons and combat training matched those of even the most elite IDF infantry and armor units. Those efforts resulted in the downing of seventy-nine Egyptian and twenty-four Syrian aircraft. In Sinai, Air Defense units defended IAF air bases faithfully, turning back

Future Air Defense gunners learn what not to shoot at as instructors display a chart illustrated with friendly *choppers.* IAF Magazine

numerous Egyptian air raids. Later in the conflict, mobile AA guns followed the advancing IDF counterattack force deep inside Egyptian territory; they encountered Egyptian pilots who, with their Mi-8s filled with napalm, attempted to fly suicide missions into pontoon bridges the Israelis had established over the Suez Canal. On the Golan Heights, AA units were rushed atop Mount Hermon, where they battled and shot down numerous Syrian jets and helicopters attempting to ferry in commando forces.

In the bitter War of Attrition that followed the United Nations imposed cease-fire on the Golan Heights, the IAF's Air Defense units deployed a new and destructive weapon into the fray: the surface-to-air version of the air-to-air Sidewinder missile—the Chaparral. In the middle of the 1973 war, the IAF sent several of its best AA officers to the United States to learn the secrets of the Chaparral; they returned to the eye of the storm nineteen days later to form a new AA battalion. On May 16, 1974, a Chaparral battery on the Golan Heights launched its missiles against a Syrian MiG-17; the MiG was obliterated without much difficulty. As with the Hawk before, the MiG-17's demise was the first kill ever for the Chaparral system.

Following the 1973 war, besides obtaining such advanced weapons systems as the Super Hawk and the M163 Vulcan 20 millimeter cannon, the IAF improved its bought-off-the-shelf "things that go bang."

The IAF's love and expertise for tinkering were poignantly illustrated in 1982, over Lebanon, when a Hawk that had been "slightly" modified by IAF technicians downed a Syrian Air Force MiG-25 Foxbat; it was believed impossible for a medium- to low-altitude SAM like the Hawk to shoot down a superspeedster high-altitude sky scorcher like the Foxbat. Such feats, in addition to its new hardware and expanded combat responsibilities, created a unique and elitist Air Defense esprit de corps.

The acquisition of the handheld Redeye SAM, which enabled Air Defense soldiers to become integral parts of infantry, paratroop, and tank units, made their combat status and responsibilities more evident. The Vulcan, on the other hand, turned the once rear Air Defense Forces into a mechanized element—a force on the cutting edge of every IDF combat operation.

The true turning point for the Air Defense Forces came in Lebanon, during Operation Peace for Galilee. That war was a conflict of firsts for the AA units. It recorded the first successful deployment of the IAF-improved Hawk (the destruction of the MiG–25) and the first kill ever recorded for the handheld Redeye.

On June 10, 1982, near the village of Ein Zehalta along the Beirut-Damascus Highway, a force of Redeye missile soldiers commanded by 1st Lt. Rami Targer was attached to a battalion of paratroopers who were battling a force of heavily armed Syrian commandos and T–62 tanks. The Redeye unit's job was to protect the paratroopers from the untimely and uninvited appearance of Syrian Gazelle or Mi–24 attack choppers; the missile soldiers dispersed into the surrounding hills and thick citrus groves to prepare a surface-to-air ambush for the enemy ships.

Something much different and much better appeared, however. As the Israeli paratroopers and Syrian commandos fought it out at close range, Targer noticed a jet that was definitely not friendly: it was a Syrian Air Force MiG–23 Flogger-E. He yelled to his legions through the unit's radio, "MiG behind us . . . I repeat, MiG behind us, prepare to launch missiles!" The missile soldiers quickly raised their Redeyes, and two were fired. The first missile failed to lock onto its target and fell in the distance. The second Redeye locked onto the Flogger-E's exhaust, chased it, and, with all eyes from the battle below now locked onto the sky above, blew it out of the sky. For Targer's unit, this was the first Israeli kill of an enemy aircraft using a handheld SAM. For General Dynamics, the makers of the Redeye, it was the first time its product had ever done what it was made for *in combat.*

The most important development for the IAF's Air Defense Forces was the development of the mobile cannons, made by combining the 20 millimeter Vulcan M61A1A cannon, the US Navy Mk. 20 Mod. O lead-computing sight and range-only radar, and the M113 APC.

The Vulcan units were the true embodiment of the Air Defense Forces as a combat organization. Its crews are subjected to full combat infantry training—with armor and infantry units in brigade- and division-size maneuvers—to inaugurate them into the art and frantic chaos of all-out, full-scale combat. Their role in battle was to provide antiaircraft fire, but, as seen in Lebanon, they'd be doing a lot more.

During the first few days of Operation Peace for Galilee, the Vulcans that were attached to the tank and infantry units racing toward Beirut faced little interference from enemy aircraft. They did encounter a determined and fanatic Palestinian enemy. The Palestinians were firmly entrenched throughout the Lebanese coastal area; their antitank and sniper dens were well hidden amid the labyrinth of shell-scarred buildings and hapless civilians of the various refugee camps around Tyre and Sidon. Rooting out these positions was a painful and costly task for the Israeli forces, especially since IDF Chief of Staff Lt. Gen. Rafael Eitan ordered that the death and suffering of innocent civilians—even if they were being used as shields—was to be avoided at all costs. Since using air power, artillery, or tank fire would be overkill, anxious company and battalion commanders frequently found themselves on the radio requesting immediate appearances from Vulcan units.

The 20 millimeter antiaircraft cannon soon proved itself to be an ideal ground-support weapon; the humming and perpetual thud of this six-barrel, 1,000 rounds per minute cannon was sweet music to pinned-down IDF infantry forces and utter terror to anyone unfortunate enough to be on the wrong side of it. The Vulcan was particularly effective against Palestinian snipers held up in buildings, obliterating a sniper's perch, the sniper's room, and much of the sniper's floor. Appreciated by every Israeli combat soldier in the field as guardian angels, the Vulcan crews were still itching for their chance to finally engage Syrian aircraft. On the armored plating of one Vulcan vehicle, for example, an overconfident crewmember had even scribbled the mocking and instigating phrase "EFOH HA'MIGIM?" "Where are the MiGs?"

The MiGs appeared on June 10 over the village of Ducha, on the outskirts of Beirut, during a vicious fire-fight between Israeli and Palestinian forces. A Vulcan battery had joined a tank unit and squad of paratroopers to battle a force of Palestinian guerrillas for control of Ducha when 1st Lt. Dubi Amitai, the battery's commander, looked in the sky and spotted a Syrian Air Force MiG-21. While incessant Palestinian machine gun and RPG fire was directed against the Israeli force, the barrels of six Vulcans were raised from minus 5 degrees, upward to the heavens at plus 85 degrees; the gunners switched on their range radars and switched their rate-of-fire selectors from the 1,000 rounds per minute of the ground role to 3,000 rounds per minute—the real thing—and began to fire.

As the explosive thuds of 20 millimeter projectiles chased the MiG, a Vulcan crewman saw several Palestinian guerrillas inching their way toward his vehicle; he immediately grabbed his GALIL assault rifle and let loose a quieting burst of 5.56 millimeter fire. By the time the soldier's GALIL magazine was empty—15 seconds to be exact—the MiG had already erupted into a massive fiery ball.

After a hearty MAZAL TOV to his battery, First Lieutenant Amitai ordered all Vulcan barrels down, their rate-of-fire selectors switched back to 1,000, and the cannons returned to the task at hand: the capture and battle of Ducha. Similar occurrences, where Vulcan crews engaged both ground and air targets, were also recorded against Syrian commando units and MiG-21s along the Beirut-Damascus Highway.

In Operation Peace for Galilee, the Hawk, Chaparral, Redeye, and Vulcan units that fought enemies both in the air and on the ground distinguished themselves. They played an integral role in the IAF's masterful victory over the Syrian Air Force and in the success of the IDF's overall military campaign. Several Air Defense soldiers were killed and dozens more wounded in the conflict, and one corporal in a Vulcan battery, Yaron Levins, was awarded the I'TUR HA'OZ, medal of valor—similar in merit and significance to the US Silver Star—for rescuing injured and burning comrades near Beirut Inter-

national Airport. According to an Air Defense officer and Lebanon veteran, "The war made us real and accepted, a true part of the big picture."

In a noted index of the world's weapons systems, the M163 Vulcan is criticized for its lack of an all-weather fire control system. All-weather had better not include the bitter cold, for otherwise the Vulcan detachment commanded by twenty-year-old Second Lieutenant Doron is in dire straits; his battery is stationed along the Purple Line, near numerous KIBBUTZIM and MOSHAVIM. The IAF has positioned Second Lieutenant Doron's unit, as well as numerous other AA forces, along the border with Lebanon for good reason: Palestinian terrorists have attempted ingenious and, on one tragic occasion, murderous attempts to cross the Purple Line, even by air. In 1979, terrorists from Abu Abbass' Palestine Liberation Front (PLF)—the same group responsible for the hijacking of the cruise ship *Achille Lauro* six years later—attempted unsuccessfully to fly into Israel using a hang glider; in 1981, terrorists from the same group attempted the same trick, only this time using a hot-air balloon. Both attacks failed in embarrassing fashion.

Then came the Night of the Hang Glider, which became a battle cry for the Air Defense units stationed in northern Israel. On November 25, 1987, a lone terrorist from the PFLP-GC—the same group responsible for the bombing of Pan Am Flight 103 over Lockerbie, Scotland—successfully evaded IAF ground radar and maneuvered his motorized hang glider into northern Israel unhindered. Instead of attacking Kiryat Shmoneh, a civilian target, the terrorist chose the GIBOR base for a NA'HA'L (a Hebrew acronym for Fighting Pioneer Youth) unit. The results were devastating and shocking; before being killed, the terrorist took six Israeli infantrymen with him. His bold action against an Israeli military installation inspired the *Intifadah*. The Night of the Hang Glider showed that Israel's frontier was most easily breached by air. This fact showed how important the Vulcans are to Israeli security.

Life for a Vulcan unit along the Purple Line is demanding, Spartan, and as front-line as it gets. The unit's soldiers patrol an area along the "fence": the heavily fortified, electronically monitored, barbed-wire and land mine separation post that declares northern Israel off-limits to all unfriendlies. While along the fence, the Vulcan units are like any other combat force in the IDF; they mount foot patrols, secure areas, and keep the civilian settlements safe from armed intruders. Their 20 millimeter rattlers, however, make them much more than foot soldiers. According to Second Lieutenant Doron, "Our principal responsibility is, of course, to insure that MiGs, enemy helicopters, balloons, hang gliders, or *even birds carrying grenades* come nowhere near the border. We are, after all, Air Force. But we are also a mobile artillery squad, giving fire support wherever and whenever it is needed. Ever since Night of the Hang Glider, we have had to carry the burden of keeping the skies clean, with the exception, of course, of our own ships. Our sector commander, Lieutenant Colonel [A.], has made it clear that *he* wouldn't want to be a soldier from the Vulcan unit which let Night of the Hang Glider *Two* take place. And we certainly believe him!"

When air force JOBNIKS joke that the Air Defense soldiers are suckers—khaki (IAF) soldiers living in green (mud-stomping, infantry) conditions—they're really talking about the Vulcan soldiers in the north. The JOBNIKS serve in air bases with swimming pools; movie theaters; gigantic dining halls; and a PX complete with after-shave, chocolates, and books. The Vulcan soldiers in the bush live in the other end of the spectrum. They eat out of a small closetlike kitchen, can buy only cigarettes and sodas in their PX, and live in tents or concrete-fortified quarters; they sleep with their weapons in damp and cold cots—that is, if they're lucky enough to be able to lay their heads on the folded winter parkas and steal some sleep at all.

Operational duty is a 24 hour per day occupation. When the winter's sky darkens into a crimson cover and a cold and bitter day becomes a brutally frigid night, "fun time" begins. The soldiers of the night watch put on their Nomex fire-retardant coverall; Air Force blue winter parkas; zippered combat boots; and the Kevlar flak vest. The web gear, an asymmetrical arrangement of ammunition pouches, is always filled to capacity with a dozen banana-shaped thirty-round magazines full of 5.56 millimeter shells for the GLILON assault rifle, as well as several antipersonnel grenades and two filled-to-capacity canteens.

Every night is tense, but tonight promises to be hot. Second Lieutenant Doron returns from the company commander's intelligence briefing apprehensive and determined. It is highly probable that a band of terrorists will attempt a border crossing tonight, and his unit will probably be in the thick of it. He gathers his men around their vehicles and goes over a map of Lebanon that is covered with plastic and decorated with numerous markings, stickers, and scribbled notations. As he points to a small spot on the map, he explains combat procedure for the umpteenth time. His men are young, but all are combat veterans. After describing the probabilities and possibilities for this evening's ambush, Second Lieutenant Doron brings out

With one hand on the Old Testament and the other on a GALIL *5.56 millimeter assault rifle, a new Air Defense soldier swears his allegiance to God, to the Israel Defense Force, and to the State of Israel.* BITON HEYL HAVIR

109

the aerial identification chart and rehashes the silhouettes of MiG–21s, 23s, 25s, 27s, and 29s; Sukhoi 7s, 20s, and 24s; and all the attack choppers in the Syrians' inventory.

A one-time pilot candidate, Doron loves the Air Force and everything involving aircraft— even if it means shooting them down. As he puts on his Kevlar crew member's helmet and climbs atop the M163, he folds his gray-blue Air Force beret and looks with great affection at its silver metal HEYL HAVIR badge with red background. After contemplating where he'd be now had he passed pilot's course, he carefully folds the beret and places it securely in his flak vest—a super-

A Hawk SAM battery in northern Israel keeps a stoic vigil against incoming enemy ordnance—from MiGs to missiles to terrorist hang gliders! BAMACHANE

stitious effort of added protection meant to ward off evil spirits and Palestinian bullets.

The vehicle's motor is started and the Vulcan heads out from home base, passing the barbed-wire fences and perimeter guard for the short ride toward the fence and the security zone inside Lebanon. The winter's rains have made the ground muddy and difficult to maneuver through, a handicap when a vehicle's mobility might save a crew from an RPG round. Weapons are cocked, the 20 millimeter cannon swung around in a 360 degree radius, raised up and down, and prepared for action. Moments later they're inside Lebanon. No one really expects to face a PLF hot-air balloon tonight or a PFLP-GC hang glider, but ever since the Night of the Hang Glider, eyes, weapons, and sights are always raised toward the heavens; not being prepared for any eventuality can be a fatal miscalculation.

Along a route secured hours earlier by a force of combat engineers, the Vulcan grinds a slow and cautious path—its treads spitting out a constant splattering of reddish mud, its exhaust polluting the crisp Levantine air with an engulfing smell of benzine. At a predetermined point, the Vulcan finds itself a home for tonight's ambush.

The crew lowers the radio's volume so its clatter isn't heard for miles around. They have nothing to do but wait and relish the quiet, which hopefully will *not* be shattered by the sounds of gunfire.

The gunner swings the cannon up and down and around, gazing into the specially attached infrared night-fighting sight. A suspicious vehicle—in Lebanon, everything that moves is suspicious to someone or another—is located in the distance, and the 20 millimeter cannon tracks it slowly. It turns out to be nothing.

Second Lieutenant Doron, sitting atop the command M113 APC, flips his one-eyed night-fighting lens across his Kevlar helmet and searches the area for any sign of trouble—both in the skies and on the ground. The terrorists are well trained and more familiar with the terrain than any Israeli soldier will ever be. They can break through at any place, through any hole.

All it takes is for one Israeli eye not to be focused for a split second, and an antitank grenade is under the vehicle.

The quiet of the ambush is deafening.

The Vulcan has been in its hiding place for almost 6 hours when the muted popping of gunfire is heard in the distance; nearby, flaming orange flares fall from the sky. Several terrorists were about to make their way toward Israeli lines when they discovered that they were in the approaches to a paratrooper ambush; the terrorists, four it is estimated, ran for dear life into a thick and mazelike field of olive trees. Because it is too risky to have the paratroopers pursue them on foot and at night, Doron's Vulcan detachment is called in for help.

The paratroopers, young, nervous, and fired up, are happy to see the Vulcan arrive. Platoon commanders with red and blue berets discuss the situation, and then Corporal Yuval, the Vulcan's gunner, is given his instructions. With the paratroopers looking on in awe, Corporal Yuval places his cannon down at a minus 2 degree angle, which will hit anyone in the area in the chest or waist; places the bright red oval gunsight on a tree being used as a marker; and rakes the field with approximately 500 rounds of 20 millimeter hellfire. The muzzle flash is mesmerizing, as is the Vulcan's destructive wrath; hundreds of trees, bushes, and whatever else is there are reduced to pulp. No wonder the infantry forces operating in the security zone call the Vulcan the heavy metal guitar of automatic weaponry.

The next morning, the paratroopers will search the field of downed tree trunks and

On frontier duty in the southern portion of Israel, batteries of M48A1 Chaparral SAMs prepare for any eventuality. BITON HEYL HAVIR

111

branches to see if the Vulcan hit anything. Second Lieutenant Doron's detachment will head back to Israel at sunrise, with the comforting orange glow of the sunshine just appearing over the snow-capped Mount Hermon in the east. As the vehicles return to base and pass the guard tower—the soldier inside searching the sky with powerful field glasses—another Vulcan will head for Lebanon, its swinging turret and erect cannon searching the heavens for targets. After some coffee and a breakfast prepared by Shirli, the company's secretary, the night watch will clean their weapons, maintain their vehicles, and, if nothing develops across the fence, throw their tired bodies onto unsleepable cots for an hour or two. According to Second Lieutenant Doron, "Our most dangerous enemy is, in fact,

monotony, and this is why patrols inside Lebanon are not only important to the security of the nearby KIBBUTZIM, but to the cohesiveness and effectiveness of the unit."

The IAF also realizes that monotony for an AA unit, especially one stationed along a frontier where it sees few enemy aircraft, is a danger and occasionally sends the Vulcans down south for large-scale maneuvers. Second Lieutenant Doron's battalion had just returned from such an exercise, where his men proved to be in superb battle-ready shape. In the mountainous desert, their Vulcan battalion protected an advance of MERKAVA MBTs, M113 APCs, and infantry soldiers from air attack. They proved especially effective against Cobra and Defender helicopter gunships, tracking the maneuverable and wily

M113 Vulcans on the march on maneuvers. Michael Zarfati, BAMACHANE

ships on their low-level attack runs until a fuselage was in the sights and, in training at least, the aircraft destroyed.

Most soldiers in the Vulcan detachment prefer service along the Purple Line to training maneuvers down south. Said Corporal Eyal, an assistant gunner and detachment communications NCO standing guard inside a sandbagged pillbox, "If I have to clean the vehicle, maintain it, grease the gun, and do the routine dirty work, [I'd] much rather ply my trade to where those activities will come to some practical use, and there is no more practical place for a Vulcan unit than here, opposite Lebanon. Of course, service here in the bunker and with our unit is absolutely exhausting, as we're on alert almost twenty-four hours a day. It's worthwhile, however, *very worthwhile!*"

A practical location for a Hawk battery is atop the Golan Heights, between Mount Hermon and Lebanon. Most experts conclude that the next major conflict is going to erupt, be fought, and be won or lost on the volcanic ash plateau so bitterly disputed between Israel and Syria. Determined not to allow any Syrian aircraft the opportunity to assist in that dreaded effort is the Hawk missile battery of Second Lieutenant Shmulik and his three-man crew of controller, radar operator, and electronics specialist. Although Hawks don't travel into Lebanon for anti-terrorist ambushes, their soldiers sometimes do; these units are like a Vulcan or any other AA unit—100 percent combat!

The Hawk battery's fire-control room, located too close to the border with Syria for comfort, is small and electronically active; it is about the size of a bathroom if the showers and sinks were replaced by hulking boxes of lights, switches, and wires. It is underground, well protected against a surface-to-surface missile hit or a surprise bombing run, obscured by a lengthy and involved camouflaged net, and armed with automatic weapons just in case any uninvited visitors come knocking at the door. On that door is a stenciled drawing of the MiG-25 Foxbat that this same battery downed during Lebanon. The Foxbat is underneath a gigantic full-color fac-simile of a bat: the Air Defense Forces unit emblem.

The control room is the nerve, as well as social, center of the Hawk battery. It is active around the clock, with all eyes and ears following a host of electronic devices and radar screens. Sometimes, one of the few female NCOs authorized to fire the Hawk serves in this battery, and her smiles and professionalism frequently break the routine of monotony and tension. Generally, however, the control chamber is filled with electrifying anxiety. One successful break in the IAF electronic shield, and a military base or a city can be decimated. Whereas IAF warplanes can respond to an enemy air attack in minutes, the Hawk's chance for an encounter with the enemy is always instantaneous; the difference between success and failure depends on the cohesive bond the crew has developed inside the claustrophobic confines of the control room.

In full battle kit, a Vulcan vehicle leaves the safe confines of Israel proper and heads across the Purple Line and straight toward myriad Palestinian terror groups and Hizbollah. Although their primary mission is air defense, joint-security operations do not differentiate between the IAF and the IDF, who, many khaki-clad HEYL HAVIR officers have argued, "aren't part of the real IAF anyway!" BITON HEYL HAVIR

Although he knows his men and women to be the best, twenty-one-year-old Second Lieutenant Shmulik is nervous, always nervous, to the very end. During the long and arduous day, Shmulik likes to venture outside the underground chamber to examine his Hawks—his babies. In the barren and rough landscape of the Golan, the white and gray Hawks stand like stoic symbols—deadly yet beautiful landmarks of vigilance and destruction. Shmulik treats every Hawk as if it were alive, although he hopes that he—and the State of Israel—will never be forced to use them in combat. "Enough wars have already been fought."

Besides hunting the elusive Syrian MiGs, another objective of the Hawk battery on the Golan Heights is to prevent airborne hostile terrorist activity.

The PLO's largest military force, *el-Fatah*—the one commanded by Yasir Arafat—has within its Order of Battle a unit known as Force 14; it is, in fact, the budding component of the Palestinian Air Force. Force 14 pilots are fanatic Arafat loyalists trained in Syria, Libya, Algeria, Iraq, and the Eastern Bloc. They are proficient in aircraft ranging from the MiG–23 to the Gazelle helicopter to Fokker transports. Since Israeli intelligence believes that several Force 14 aircraft are well hidden in the Lebanese mountains, the IAF's biggest fear is that the Palestinians will one day use a civilian transport or small airliner crammed with high explosives to crash a suicide aircraft-bomb into a northern Israeli city. Such an attack, should it succeed, would result in the death of hundreds of Israeli citizens, and Second Lieutenant Shmulik's battery is determined not to let that happen. Every blip on the radar, no matter how big or fast it is, is treated as a legitimate target that directly threatens Israeli territory. Every Hawk missile operator alive would give her or his right arm to be able to shoot down one of *those* aircraft.

Every once in a while, a Hawk battery is lucky enough to get to fire the real thing. The honor of firing a real—$250,000, or 500,000 shekel—missile is a celebration of the highest kind in the vocabulary of the Air Defense Forces. For today's firing of a Hawk, at a missile range somewhere in southern Israel, the missile has been painted red and the target isn't a MiG–29, but a target drone launched toward the safe proving grounds of the Mediterranean Sea. With the invited top-brass guests observing the about-to-be-launched Hawk from a safe distance, the missile battery's fire controller tracks the target and locks onto it. "Three, Two . . . One . . . FIRE!" The missile launcher releases one of its

Wearing a Kevlar ballistic helmet, a Kevlar flak vest, load-bearing equipment filled with ammunition, and ear plugs, an Air Defense NCO demonstrates firing a captured, perhaps ex-Syrian, ex-Egyptian, or ex-Palestinian, Soviet-produced handheld SAM–7 Grail. BITON HEYL HAVIR

three Hawks. Seconds afterward, the target drone receives a direct hit from the warhead and disintegrates. The successful exercise is enjoyed the most by the conscript, who after months of training and operational assignments, gets a chance to destroy so much valued hardware in less than a minute and outside the confines of the simulator. After the firing, a boisterous Lieutenant Colonel M., the Hawk unit's commander, said, "We can *easily* shoot down any Syrian aircraft which attempts to penetrate Israeli airspace."

One Syrian aircraft that the IAF didn't succeed in shooting down, luckily, was a MiG-23-B flown by Major Bassem on October 11, 1989. Instead of attacking Israel, however, Major Bassem was a defector, wishing to flee Syria and seek political asylum in Israel. Although an intelligence coup of unimaginable proportions, the defection of the MiG-23 illustrated a severe failure in the IAF's aerial shield. Major Bassem had flown his MiG-23, with its twin 23 millimeter cannons fully loaded, over Israel for over 8 minutes at low altitude before landing at a civilian

Having proven itself during the 1973 Yom Kippur War as an effective low-level air defense system, a captured Egyptian ZSU-23-4 quadruple 23 milli- *meter AA system shows it can still provide deadly firepower, even in IAF hands.* BITON HEYL HAVIR

airfield, in Megiddo, and surrendering his aircraft to a puzzled farmer who had to contact the IAF from a pay phone!

On Monday, January 29, 1990, the MiG-23 that Major Bassem brought the Jewish State was airborne once again, at a heavily guarded, though festive, airfield in central Israel. This time, however, it sported the blue IAF Star of David emblem and was flown by Lieutenant Colonel A., the IAF's chief test pilot.

The three-month delay in bringing the MiG up for its maiden flight in the Israeli skies was due to several difficulties, most important being the time needed to build a proper maintenance support system and obtain spare parts. Oil and fuel also had to be adapted. The intimate knowledge needed to fly the MiG-23 was gladly supplied by Major Bassem.

As the MiG-23 began its takeoff approach, the IAF's top brass, men used to the most spectacular and death-defying operations, seemed nervous and anxious, but Lieutenant Colonel A.'s sharp and dramatic liftoff alleviated everyone's concern. His flight was followed by two aircraft—the F-15 and F-16—that in the past had made a career of downing MiG-23s. After several midair maneuvers that left everyone at the air base in awe, the unlikely trio flew over the nation's capital, Jerusalem; the F-15 and F-16 were "shown up" several times by the Soviet-produced fighter.

Lieutenant Colonel A., who in Lebanon downed two Syrian MiG-21s, enjoyed the flight immensely. After drying himself off from the obligatory buckets of water that follow every solo flight in a new craft, he said he was impressed by some of the MiG's capabilities and avionics systems.

In 1991, the Air Defense Forces would have the opportunity to once again defend Israel's skies, but this time the action wasn't over the Lebanese frontier or at some isolated frontier outpost. The skies the NUN-MEM units were tasked with defending were over Tel Aviv. During the tense days prior to the outbreak of the Gulf War there was a saying in Israel which summed up the nation's fear of Iraqi chemical attack, "ATA MUCHAN, ATA MUGAN" or "If you're prepared, your protected". Israel, however, wasn't really prepared. When, to a live worldwide audiance thanks to CNN, Tel Aviv and Haifa were rocked by Scud attacks in the early morning hours of January 17, 1991, Israel had no answer. Forty-eight hours later, however, the true hero of the war arrived. In a historic decision, the Israeli government allowed US forces—sent in from Germany—to bring Patriot SAMs to protect Israel's cities from Iraqi missiles; the IAF had decided to obtain the Patriot a year earlier but its crews had yet to complete their training in the United States and the missile batteries ordered had yet to arrive by the time the war erupted.

The arrival of the Patriots and their American crews was the first time since 1956 that foreign forces operated on Israeli soil, yet the American Patriot crews were warmly received by the beseiged Israeli public. In fact, many of the Patriot batteries were jointly operated by American and Israeli crews, a feat, along with the fact that many of the thirty-nine Iraqi Scuds launched at Israel were intercepted, which the commander of Air Defense Forces, Brig. Gen. Uri Ram considered a remarkable achievement of cooperation and proficiency. (The Dutch also sent several batteries of Patriot SAMs.)

According to Captain Y., commander of a Patriot battery stationed somewhere in the Tel Aviv area, "I have served along all of Israel's frontiers and have seen combat in Lebanon but never have I had such an important assignment. The missiles that landed in Ramat Gan and caused so much damage hit very close to where I live, and if there is anything within my power to prevent one of Saddam's Scuds from harming Israel—I'll destroy the projectile in midair. You can be sure of that!"

Following the war, when Americans left and gas masks and sealed rooms were all but forgotton, Israel launched the anti-ballistic missile of the next century, the indigenously produced CHETZ, or "arrow". Hopefully, it will never have to be used but, with Syria, Iran and Libya acquiring missiles ten times as advanced as the Scud, its presence will be reassuring.

Aircraft Glossary

In its forty-plus years of existence, the HEYL HAVIR, through either desperation or luxury, has flown dozens of combat and transport aircraft—from prop-driven relics to helicopters and jets. Some aircraft, like the Mosquito, were obsolete and aged warhorses even by the time the IAF received them. Others, like the F–15, are so technologically advanced and loved by their pilots that they will remain in service well into the twenty-first century. Space does not afford the mention of every aircraft that has carried the Star of David emblem. The aircraft listed below are those that are currently used by the IAF.

Dassault Mystere IV-A and Super-Mystere B-2 Storm

The IAF received the Mystere IV-A in April 1956 and the Super-Mystere in 1958—the Super-Mystere being its first supersonic aircraft. During the October-November 1956 Sinai Campaign, Mystere IV-As shot down seven Egyptian aircraft, and in 1967, they performed brilliantly as ground-attack craft. The Super-Mysteres, following the arrival of the Mirage IIIC, were used primarily for ground attack, although one bomb-laden Super-Mystere did shoot down two Egyptian MiG-21s in a dogfight during the Six Day War. Later, the Super-Mysteres were re-engined and upgunned before being removed from active service. According to foreign sources, aging Mystere IV-As and Super-Mystere B-2s are still being deployed operationally as ECM aircraft.

Poter Air CM-170 Fouga Magister TZUKIT

The Fouga Magister is the one common denominator of all IAF fighter pilots, being the first jet flown by pilot cadets, their first solo, and the sole aircraft of the IAF's aerobatic team. During the 1967 war, the TZUKITS, dressed in a nifty camouflage scheme, proved to be much more than just jet trainers, strafing and rocketing Egyptian convoys. They were deathtraps to those unfortunate enough to be hit by ground fire, however, as they had no ejection seat provisions.

Dassault Mirage IIIC

Few relationships between human and military machine have ever been as successful, as important, and as awesome as the marriage between the delta-wing Mach 2 Mirage IIIC and

A missile and an aircraft not to be crossed: the AIM–9L/M Sidewinder and the F–16 Falcon—the IAF's cutting edge. BITON HEYL HAVIR

117

An air-superiority fighter, a fighter bomber, and, according to foreign reports, an ECM aircraft: the Dassault Super-Mystere B–2. After playing a significant role in the IAF's brilliant victory of 1967, it was refitted with a stronger American engine and renamed SA'AR, "Storm."

The young driver of an F–16D checks with his ground crew chief for the much-anticipated "thumbs up!"

Note the multibarrel 20 millimeter cannon located in the aircraft's fuselage. BITON HEYL HAVIR

the IAF. The acquisition of the Mirage in 1962 elevated the IAF into a whole new stratosphere, pushing its pilots and its capabilities to fantastic dimensions. The silver aircraft became as much a symbol of Israel's epic 1967 victory as were the reunification of Jerusalem and the act of Israeli soldiers swimming in the Suez Canal. During the 1967 war, the Mirage was Israeli air superiority, proving second to none in air-to-air combat, as well as in a ground-attack role. It would, in fact, be hard to find a single IAF Mirage with no victory roundels painted on its fuselage; several Mirages have even accounted for double ace honors, and two Mirages, numbers 111 and 159, share the national record with thirteen enemy kills each. The Mirage proved so successful that IAI emulated its shape, performance, and impact with the development of, first, the NESHER and, later, the KFIR family.

McDonnell Douglas A-4 Skyhawk

If there were ever an IAF dictionary, then under the word *workhorse* would be a photo of the A-4 Skyhawk. Short on size, weight, and cost,

A new generation has indeed dawned—even if it is short-lived. Led by a KFIR *C-7, two newly christened* LAVI *fighter-bombers, numbers B-1 and B-2, make their maiden flight above thousands of cheering Israelis, on December 31, 1986.* Yoav Efrati

the Skyhawk was long on performance; it served for the IAF in the War of Attrition, the Yom Kippur War, and Operation Peace for Galilee and continues to serve with honor, pounding targets with distinction in antiterrorist campaigns in Lebanon. Procured in greater quantities and variants than any other aircraft in IAF history, the Skyhawk was modified by IAI for front-line service well beyond its design life. A strong and reliable bomber, the Skyhawk will always be remembered for its May 12, 1970, air-to-air battle over *Fatahland* in Lebanon. That day, a Skyhawk, busily engaged in a bombing and strafing run against Palestinian terrorist targets, shot down an intervening Syrian MiG-17 Fresco with an antitank rocket—probably the only such air-to-air kill ever recorded. The hit was so successful and destructive that the London *Daily Express* printed an article the following day insinuating that the IAF had developed a "secret" weapon.

McDonnell Douglas F-4 Phantom

What the Mirage did for the IAF in the early sixties, the Phantom did for it in the late sixties, the seventies, the eighties, the nineties and—as

The IAF's newest addition: a MiG-23 Flogger-B, preparing to take off from a base in central Israel for its maiden flight in IAF colors. IDF spokesman

has been seen with the 600 plus modifications made to the aircraft and with the maiden flight of the Phantom 2000 in August 1987—into the twenty-first century, as well. When the veteran F–4E was first received in 1969, it was the IAF's first true multirole combat aircraft, proving equally outstanding in a ground-attack role, where it can carry an external ordnance load of up to 16,000 lb, and as an air-superiority ship; it was maneuverable, agile, speedy, and deadly. The F–4E has participated in some of the IAF's most memorable battles, including the downing of five Soviet-piloted MiG-21s over the Suez Canal; the bombing of Syrian Military Headquarters in Damascus during the 1973 war; and the bombing of Beirut in 1982. During the early seventies, the A–4 Skyhawk, the Mirage IIIC, and the Phantom made up a powerful triumvirate of aerial mastery that no Arab air force could succeed in countering. In the early nineties, the Phantom was still in a triumvirate of aerial might, although it now shared billing with the F–15 and the F–16.

Before a "routine" antiterrorist patrol above the Mediterranean, a pilot and his trusted second make their way toward their highly regarded Dornier Do–28B–1 STOL light utility aircraft. On May 30, 1990, Dorniers, such as the one pictured here, participated in the joint IDF Navy and IAF interdiction of a seaborne Palestine Liberation Front terror squad heading for the crowded Tel Aviv beach area. Sivan Farag', IDF spokesman

Israel Aircraft Industries NESHER

When Israel launched its silencing preemptive strike against its Arab neighbors on June 5, 1967, France, its largest arms supplier, declared an all-inclusive arms embargo against the Jewish State. At the time, however, the IAF had already paid for fifty Mirage V fighters, and it was determined at all costs to obtain its aircraft—French embargo or not. According to foreign sources, through a brilliant intelligence operation involving the MOSSAD and a Swiss firm that built the Mirage under license for the Swiss Air Force, the blueprints for the Mirage were stolen and the aircraft was built in Israel. The resulting warplane, combining the ingenious French design and Israeli modifications, was called the NESHER, "Eagle," and was first rolled out in early 1970; it was promptly placed in a Mirage squadron and proved to be the precursor to the KFIR. The NESHER recorded its first kill during the 1973 war, when an example blew a Syrian MiG-21 out of the sky with a SHAFRIR, "homemade," air-to-air missile.

Israel Aircraft Industries KFIR C-1, C-2, TC-2, and C-7

The advent of the Mach 2+ KFIR fighter-bomber, an Israeli-produced aerial masterpiece, was a tangible response to Israel's historic reliance on unreliable arms suppliers. On April 14, 1976, in the footsteps of the Mirage and its forefather, the NESHER, the first two KFIR fighter-bombers were unveiled to the public; they were, basically, a French aircraft with an American engine complemented by Israeli ingenuity. The KFIR C-2, with its fixed canard wings and aerodynamic modifications, was highly maneuverable and extremely agile in dogfights. With seven hard underwing points, the KFIR C-2 was a potent ground-attack ship, able to carry almost 10,000 lb of ordnance. The KFIR's first kill occurred on April 27, 1979, when a joint F-15 and KFIR patrol of southern Lebanon met a flight of Syrian MiG-21s; a KFIR blew one of the MiGs out of the sky. KFIRS have participated in all of Israel's military operations since 1976, performing tasks that range from bombing Lebanon to escorting the plane carrying Egyptian president

Anwar as-Sadat to Israel. The first KFIR C-7, a KFIR for the nineties, was handed over to the IAF in July 1983. Although the KFIR will be phased out of IAF service in the nineties, it will be, according to a senior IAF pilot, "not because our lion cub wasn't good, but because something *better* came along." Today, the KFIR—or a homegrown variant—flies in Ecuador and in South Africa, where it's known as the Cheetah.

McDonnell Douglas F-15 Eagle

What the Mirage was to IAF air-to-air superiority in the sixties, the F-15 Eagle, perhaps one of the most advanced fighters ever produced, was to the IAF in the eighties. Fast, maneu-

verable, and deadly, the F-15 participated in some important and spectacular military operations, including the destruction of the Iraqi nuclear reactor in Baghdad on June 7, 1981; the war in Lebanon; and the October 1985 bombing of PLO Headquarters in Tunis. The F-15 also scored the world's first MiG-25 Foxbat kill, shooting it down over Lebanon on February 13, 1981. The tenacity of the F-15 was illustrated in the skies over Lebanon during Operation Peace for Galilee when, in an 8.5 G-force dogfight with a MiG-23, an F-15 piloted by Major (Reserves) R. was struck by an air-to-air missile seconds after it had destroyed the MiG that fired the missile. The missile exploded in the right engine's ex-

Needing only a small opening in which to land his ship, a Bell-212 pilot practices air base parking in southern Israel. BITON HEYL HAVIR

haust pipe, punching a large hole through the aircraft; 400 additional holes were caused by shrapnel, damaging the left engine and the compressor, as well. Nevertheless, Major R. landed his ship without incident.

General Dynamics F-16 A, B, C, and D Falcon

In a 1990 issue of the IAF's magazine BITON HEYL HAVIR, the bible for Israeli air enthusiasts, the F-16 Falcon was voted by IAF air crews as the "plane of the decade," with all variants receiving thirty-nine percent of the total vote. The first four F-16s reached Israel on July 2, 1980, and they've been blazing a path across the Middle Eastern skies ever since. Long regarded as a compact package of technical wizardry, the F-16 made an IAF name for itself on June 7, 1981, when a flight of Falcons destroyed the Osirak nuclear reactor near Baghdad. Two months earlier, in support of a besieged Christian position in Lebanon, an F-16 shot down a Syrian Mi-8. On July 14, 1981, during a "routine"

An IAF AH-1S Cobra helicopter gunship performs a sharp turn above the heads of a MERKAVA *Mk.II crew.* IDF spokesman

122

patrol of southern Lebanon, the F-16 scored its first kill of an enemy fighter when Colonel A.'s ship blew a Syrian MiG-21 out of the sky. The kill came fifteen years to the day after an IAF Mirage bagged its first kill. During Operation Peace for Galilee, the F-16 played an integral role in the destruction of the Syrian SAM labyrinth. The F-16 also executed the farthest-reaching Israeli military operation when a flight of Falcons bombed and destroyed PLO Headquarters in Tunis, Tunisia, on October 1, 1985.

Israel Aircraft Industries LAVI

The IAI's attempt to produce a technologically superior, indigenously conceived and designed answer to the F-16 was ambitious. Building the LAVI, "Young Lion," required a coordinated effort of Israel's most able minds, as well as a large portion of the Israeli defense budget—all supported and subsidized by American financial aid. On December 31, 1986, amid great public fanfare not seen in Israel since Entebbe, the LAVI made its first flight; it was joined in midair by a flight of homegrown KFIRS. The aircraft that was to bring the IAF into the twenty-first century was downed by its sheer financial drain on the Israeli defense budget. Nevertheless, in October 1989, the third prototype of the LAVI, the B-3, made its maiden flight—unfortunately more as an advertisement for advanced Israeli-made avionics than as a hope that the aircraft would ever be produced. According to *Jane's All the World Aircraft*, IAI has compromised its quest for producing the ultraexpensive LAVI by building the NAMER, "Leopard," an aircraft with the body of the Mirage but the avionics of the LAVI.

Sikorsky S-55 and Sikorsky S-58

The American-made Sikorsky chopper was the first heavy transport helicopter in the IAF. It made a name for itself during the 1967 war when the S-58 squadron ferried an entire paratroop brigade into Sinai, at night, to capture the Egyptian fortress at Um Katef. A few days later, the S-58s transported that same brigade north, toward Syria and the capture of the Golan Heights.

Sud.Aviation (Aerospatiale) SA-321-K Super Frelon

The "big daddy" of transport choppers for many years in the IAF, the Super Frelon achieved lasting fame in Israeli folklore when it silently, efficiently, and safely transported a force of paratroop commandos to Beirut International Airport on December 28, 1968, in Operation Gift and a force of reconnaissance paratroopers to an electric powerplant deep in the Egyptian Nile Delta on November 1, 1968, in Operation Shock.

Bell-205

No Israeli veteran of the bitter guerrilla war waged in the Jordan Valley during the War of Attrition—whether a reconnaissance paratrooper or a Bedouin tracker—will ever forget the impact the light and maneuverable Bell-205s had on the IDF's ability to win the campaign. Often flying into hails of small arms fire, the camouflaged Bell-205 flew countless sorties in all conditions, at night and during the day. It participated in the 1968 raid on Beirut, and its courageous pilots executed dozens of rescue operations of downed pilots and wounded soldiers during the 1973 war. To many Bell-205

pilots who flew in the Jordan Valley, their most vivid memory is of Brig. Gen. Raful Eitan volunteering himself to antiterrorist sorties and then demanding, as only generals can, the opportunity to serve as door gunner.

Sikorsky CH-53 YASUR

From October 17, 1969, when the first two CH-53s arrived in Israel, the YASUR has made an important mark on Israeli military history. The combat operations that YASURS have participated in are a "who's who" of spectacular IDF missions, including "kidnapping" a Soviet P-12 surface-to-air radar on December 27, 1969; rescuing downed pilots deep behind enemy lines; transporting commando forces to the Syrian heartland in 1973; ferrying Israeli paratroopers to the outskirts of Beirut in 1982; and then gladly bringing thousands of Israeli soldiers *out* of Lebanon in Operation Maginot Line. Perhaps the YASUR's most famous tale of guts and glory occurred during the 1973 war, on October 9,

A CH-53 YASUR recovers an unmanned drone gone astray somewhere in southern Israel. Gil Arbel, BITON HEYL HAVIR

A Sikorsky S-58 helicopter, the first effective heavy transport chopper the IAF obtained, practices the art of plucking downed pilots from the water—the Mediterranean, in this case—with a group of naval commandos, just before the 1967 war. IDF Archives

1973, when four Egyptian MiG-21s and four Sukhoi 7s confronted a lone CH-53 flying over Sinai. For over 4 minutes, the eight Egyptian aircraft tried, but failed, to blow the YASUR out of the sky. They fired their cannons and rockets at the CH-53, but did not inflict any serious damage.

Bell-206 Jet Ranger and -206L Long Ranger

What the TZUKIT is to the future aces of the IAF, the Bell-206 is to the future pilots of helicopter gunships. The Bell-206 became an indispensable tool for the Artillery Corps as an artillery spotter, and in Israeli joint-security patrols, it pursues terrorist units.

Bell-212

The beating rat-a-tat of an airborne Bell-212, its side-door FN MAG gunners peering out into the distance, became as much a part of the Lebanese landscape as the Beirut skyline and the misery of the wartorn land. The IAF's aerial taxicab, the Bell-212 has become the most

Dressed in Syrian Air Force camouflage colors and sporting both Syrian Air Force and IAF emblems, a Gazelle tank killer chopper captured in Lebanon's Beka'a Valley during Operation Peace for Galilee prepares to land at an air base in central Israel. IDF spokesman

ubiquitous chopper in the current IAF Order of Battle. A favorite among the commando-medics of the IAF's AEU, this is the aircraft hundreds of Israeli soldiers hit by enemy fire owe their lives to.

Bell AH-1G and AH-1S Cobra

The cause of great fear and panic to any Syrian tank soldier or PLO gunner, the Cobra proved that a flying ship capable of numerous combat roles did not have to cost millions of dollars and fly at the speed of sound. Specially designed as a tank killer, the Cobra was deadly in Lebanon where it would appear from behind a protective screen of trees, fly in at top speed toward convoys of enemy vehicles, and, in a flurry of TOW missile releases and 20 millimeter barrages, turn armor into flaming heaps of twisted metal. The Cobra's favorite missions were against Palestinian naval targets, enjoying the chance to snipe away at small fishing vessels used for amphibious attacks with their TOWs and rockets.

Hughes M-D 500 Defender

Compact, nimble, and, with its four TOW missiles, deadly, the Defenders, together with the Cobra, were a powerful low-flying one-two antitank punch. Most noted for its ability to fly at low level, the tenacious Defender left many a Soviet-built MBT in flames in the tank battle-fields of the Beka'a Valley and the Beirut-Damascus Highway. Following Operation Peace for Galilee, Defenders performed "public relations" missions along the Israeli coastline, flying over crowded beaches with another attack chopper, a captured Syrian Gazelle.

Aerospatiale AS-365 *Dauphin*

Although a new arrival in the IAF family of helicopters, the Dolphin was the first shipborne aircraft; it uses the small deck of an IDF Navy ALIYAH-class missile boat as a mini aircraft carrier.

Piper Cub

The aircraft flown by more IAF pilots than any other—owing to its role in pilot's course—

the Piper Cub has been in HEYL HAVIR service since 1948. In six major wars and over forty years of hostilities, a Piper Cub variant has flown supplies, ferried generals here and there, rescued pilots, and, most important, served as a stepping stone for hundreds of future IAF aces.

Lockheed C–130 Hercules

On July 4, 1976, the day the United States celebrated its bicentennial, four American-made C–130 Hercules returned to Israel from the legendary hostage-rescue operation at Entebbe, Uganda, and became forever endeared as full-fledged citizens of the State of Israel. Through a difficult and lengthy flight course, the Hercules fleet flew 2,200 miles into deepest Africa, to Entebbe, and, then under fire, back to Israel with 103 former hostages. The Hercules' history in Israeli colors has been long and industrious; IAF C–130s have flown to Beirut in combat, as well as to Armenia and, most recently, Romania to bring in humanitarian aid during peace. Paratroopers who fly in the mammoth craft during training will forever imagine what it must have been like being a paratrooper in 1976, flying toward Entebbe.

The SAM's greatest nemesis: the AGM–78 Standard Arm "Purple Punch" antiradiation missile, which proved its lethality during the IAF's epic blitz of the Beka'a Valley missile network in June 1982. *Michael Zarfati, IDF spokesman*

Boeing 707

A member of the IAF since 1973, the Boeing 707 has been part of a fleet of aircraft used in a wide assortment of roles. Although transport craft, several Boeings have been refitted for service as aerial tankers. Several have become airborne electronic warfare and flying command posts—according to foreign sources, hovering over Tunis in April 1988, supervising and electronically protecting the operation that assassinated Abu Jihad. The aircraft owns several special distinctions in IAF history: in January 1978, it was the first IAF aircraft to ever land—voluntarily—in Egypt, and on December 11, 1988, a Boeing 707 became the first IAF aircraft to ever land in the Soviet Union in earthquake-ravaged Armenia, loaded with medical and humanitarian supplies.

Grumman OV-1 Mohawk

Although the Mohawks were unveiled only in July 1982—during the height of Operation Peace for Galilee—the IAF has operated two for reconnaissance and electronic intelligence work. With its side-looking radar and infrared sensors, it is understandable why the security-conscious IAF kept the Mohawk under wraps, although this led to imaginative speculation about what type of ops the Mohawk actually had participated in.

Grumman E-2C Hawkeye

Lost in the glory of the F-15, F-16, and KFIR is an important IAF acquisition: the Grumman E-2C Hawkeye. An all-weather, day or night AWACS aircraft with a rotating radar with a range of 250 miles, the Hawkeye is the State of Israel's airborne eyes and ears. The ability to see enemy air activity from beyond the Israeli boundaries is an invaluable strategic asset. Hawkeye pilots are chosen from among the best transport aircraft flyers and served an important role during the 1982 war, when Hawkeye pilots and radar operators directed numerous chaotic and sometimes crowded aerial dogfights between Israeli and Syrian aircraft.

Israel Aircraft Industries Sea-Scan 1124

The executive jet homegrown in the land of the blue and white, the Sea-Scan (originally known as the Westwind 1123) turned maritime patrol craft is to the IDF Navy—although in IAF control—what the Hawkeye is to the HEYL HAVIR; with its combined crew of two IAF and three IDF Navy personnel, it is an airborne model for "combined arms." Fitted with the powerful Litton radar, the Sea-Scans patrol the Mediterranean against enemy activity from the Syrian shore to the Algerian approaches.

Index

About the Author

Samuel M. Katz was born in 1963 and served in the Israel Defense Forces at the height of Israel's involvement in Lebanon. He has had a life-time interest in Israeli military matters and has written over a dozen books and articles on the subject, including *Israel's Army, Arab Armies of the Middle East Wars, Israeli Tank Battles*, and *Follow Me: A History of Israel's Military Elite.* Katz has recently completed *Guards without Frontiers*, a study of Israel's war against terrorism, and is currently at work on a POWER Series title for Motorbooks International on the Israeli Special Forces.